DOMESDAY BOOK

Middlesex

History from the Sources

DOMESDAY BOOK

A Survey of the Counties of England

LIBER DE WINTONIA

Compiled by direction of

KING WILLIAM I

Winchester
1086

DOMESDAY BOOK

text and translation edited by

JOHN MORRIS

11

Middlesex

edited from a draft translation prepared by

Sara Wood

PHILLIMORE
Chichester
1975

1975
Published by
PHILLIMORE & CO. LTD.,
London and Chichester

Head Office: Shopwyke Hall,
Chichester, Sussex, England

© John Morris, 1975

ISBN 0 85033 131 5

Printed in Great Britain by
Titus Wilson & Son Ltd.
Kendal

MIDDLESEX

History from the Sources
General Editor: John Morris

The series aims to publish history
written directly from the sources
for all interested readers, specialists
and others. The first priority is to
publish important texts which should
be widely available, but are not.

DOMESDAY BOOK

The contents, with the folio on which each county begins, are:

Domesday Book is termed *Liber de Wintonia* (The Book of Winchester) in column 332c

INTRODUCTION

The Domesday Survey

In 1066 Duke William of Normandy conquered England. He was crowned King, and most of the lands of the English nobility were soon granted to his followers. Domesday Book was compiled 20 years later. The Saxon Chronicle records that in 1085

> at Gloucester at midwinter ... the King had deep speech with his counsellors ... and sent men all over England to each shire ... to find out ... what or how much each landholder held ... in land and livestock, and what it was worth ... The returns were brought to him.[1]

William was thorough. One of his Counsellors reports that he also sent a second set of Commissioners 'to shires they did not know, where they were themselves unknown, to check their predecessors' survey, and report culprits to the King.[2]

The information was collected at Winchester, corrected, abridged, chiefly by omission of livestock and the 1066 population, and fair-copied by one writer into a single volume. Norfolk, Suffolk and Essex were copied, by several writers, into a second volume, unabridged, which states that 'the Survey was made in 1086'. The surveys of Durham and Northumberland, and of several towns, including London, were not transcribed, and most of Cumberland and Westmorland, not yet in England, was not surveyed. The whole undertaking was completed at speed, in less than 12 months, though the fair-copying of the main volume may have taken a little longer. Both volumes are now preserved at the Public Record Office. Some versions of regional returns also survive. One of them, from Ely Abbey,[3] copies out the Commissioners' brief. They were to ask

> The name of the place; Who held it, before 1066, and now? How many *hides*?[4]
> How many ploughs, both those in lordship and the men's?
> How many villagers, cottagers and slaves, how many free men and Freemen?[5]
> How much woodland, meadow and pasture? How many mills and fishponds?
> How much has been added or taken away? What the total value was and is?
> How much each free man or Freeman had or has? All threefold, before 1066,
>   when King William gave it, and now; and if more can be had than at present?

The Ely volume also describes the procedure. The Commissioners took evidence on oath 'from the Sheriff; from all the barons and their Frenchmen; and from the whole Hundred, the priests, the reeves and six villagers from each village'. It also names four Frenchmen and four Englishmen from each Hundred, who were sworn to verify the detail.

The King wanted to know what he had, and who held it. The Commissioners therefore listed lands in dispute, for Domesday Book was not only a tax-assessment. To the King's grandson, Bishop Henry of Winchester, its purpose was that every 'man should know his right and not

---

[1] Before he left England for the last time, late in 1086.
[2] Robert Losinga, Bishop of Hereford 1079-1095 (see *E.H.R.* 22, 1907, 74).
[3] *Inquisitio Eliensis*, folio 1a.
[4] A land unit.
[5] *Quot liberi homines? Quot sochemani?*

usurp another's'; and because it was the final authoritative register of rightful possession 'the natives called it Domesday Book, by analogy from the Day of Judgement'; that was why it was carefully arranged by Counties, and by landholders within Counties, 'numbered consecutively ... for easy reference'.[6]

Domesday Book describes Old English society under new management, in minute statistical detail. Foreign lords had taken over, but little else had yet changed. The chief landholders and those who held from them are named, and the rest of the population was counted. Most of them lived in villages, whose houses might be clustered together, or dispersed among their fields. Villages were grouped in administrative districts called Hundreds, which formed regions within Shires, or Counties, which survive today with minor boundary changes; the recent deformation of some ancient county identities is here disregarded, as are various short-lived modern changes. The local assemblies, though overshadowed by lords great and small, gave men a voice, which the Commissioners heeded. Very many holdings were described by the Norman term *manerium* (manor), greatly varied in size and structure from tiny farmsteads to vast holdings; and many lords exercised their own jurisdiction and other rights, termed *soca*, whose meaning still eludes exact definition.

The survey was unmatched in Europe for many centuries, the product of a sophisticated and experienced English administration, fully exploited by the Conqueror's commanding energy. But its unique assemblage of facts and figures has been hard to study, because the text has not been easily available, and abounds in technicalities. Investigation has therefore been chiefly confined to specialists; a wide range of questions cannot be tackled adequately without a cheap text and uniform translation available to a wider range of students, including local historians.

Previous Editions

The text of the two volumes has been printed once, in 1783 by Abraham Farley, in an edition of 1,250 copies, at Government cost, originally estimated at £18,000 exclusive of salaries. Its preparation took 16 years. It was set in a specially designed type, destroyed by fire in 1808, here reproduced from the original edition. In 1816 the Records Commissioners added two more volumes, edited by Sir Henry Ellis, of introduction, indices, and associated text; and in 1861-1863 the Ordnance Survey issued zincograph facsimiles of the whole. Separate texts of many counties have appeared since 1673 and separate translations in the Victoria County Histories and elsewhere.

This Edition

Farley's text is used, because of its excellence, and because any worthy alternative would prove astronomically expensive. His text has been checked against the facsimile, and discrepancies observed have been

6 *Dialogue de Scaccario*, 1, 16.

verified against the manuscript, by the kindness of Miss Daphne Gifford of the Public Record Office. Farley's few errors are indicated in the notes.

The editor is responsible for the translation and lay-out. It aims at what the compiler would have written if his language had been modern English; though no translation can be exact, for even a simple word like 'free' nowadays means freedom from different restrictions. Bishop Henry emphasized that his grandfather preferred 'ordinary words'; the nearest ordinary modern English is therefore chosen whenever possible. Words that are now obsolete, or have changed their meaning, are avoided, but measurements have to be transliterated, since their extent is often unknown or arguable, and varied regionally. The terse inventory form of the original has been retained, as have the ambiguities of the Latin.

Modern English commands two main devices unknown to 11th-century Latin: standardised punctuation and paragraphs. Latin *ibi* (there are) is usually rendered by a full stop, Latin *et* (and) by a comma or semi-colon. The entries normally answer the Commissioners' questions, arranged in five main groups, (i) the place and its holder, its hides, ploughs and lordship; (ii) people; (iii) resources; (iv) value; and (v) additional notes. These groups are usually given as separate paragraphs.

King William numbered chapters 'for easy reference', and sections within chapters are commonly marked, usually by initial capitals, often edged in red. They are here numbered, for ease of reference only. Maps, indices and an explanation of technical terms are also given. Later, it is hoped to publish full analytical tables, an explanatory volume, and associated texts.

The editor is deeply indebted to the advice of many scholars, too numerous to name, and especially to the Public Record Office, and to the publisher's patience. The draft translations are the work of a team; they have been co-ordinated and corrected by the editor, and each has been checked by several people. It is therefore hoped that mistakes may be fewer than in versions published by single fallible individuals. But it would be Utopian to hope that the translation is altogether free from error; the editor would therefore like to be informed of mistakes observed.

Huntingdonshire, Middlesex and Surrey have been the experimental counties at all stages of this edition. They may therefore contain more ineptitudes and mistakes than other counties.

The texts have been set by Sheila Brookshire, Jill Doig, Yvonne Grant, Auriol Hyde Parker, Isobel Thompson and Elizabeth Thorneycroft. The map is the work of Jim Hardy.

Conventions

*	refers to a note.
[ ]	enclose words omitted in the MS.
( )	enclose editorial explanations.

126 d

HIC ANNOTANT TENENTES TRAS IN MIDDELSEXE.

.I.REX WILLELMVS.

.II.Archieps cantuariens.

.III.Eps Lundon 7 Canonici ej.

.IIII.Abbatia de Weftmonaft.

.V.Abbatia S Kinitat Rotom.

.VI.Abbatia de Berchinges.

.VII.Comes Rogerius.

.VIII Comes Moritoniens.

.IX.Goisfrid de Manneuile.

.X.Ernulf de Hefding.

.XI.Walteri filius Other.

XII.Walteri de S Walarico.

.XIII.Ricard filius Gifebti comit.

.XIIII.Robertus Gernon.

.XV.Robertus Fafiton.

.XVI.Robtus filius Rozelini.

.XVII.Robertus blundus.

.XVIII.Rogerius de Rames.

.XIX.Willelmus filius Anfculf.

.XX.Eduuard de Sarifberie.

.XXI.Albericus de Ver.

.XXII.Rannulfus fr Ilger.

XXIII.Derman

XXII.Judita comitiſa. 7 Elemofinar regis.

127 a

IN OSVLVESTANE Hundret . tenet Wills rex
XII . acs træ 7 dim de nanefmaneflande . H tra ua
luit 7 ualet . v . fol . hac habuit rex EDW fimilit.
In eod hund ht rex . xxx . cot.   qui reddun
p annu xIIII . fol 7 x . den 7 I . obolu.
Ad Holeburne ht rex . II . cot q reddunt p annu
.xx . den uicecomiti regis.   T.R.E.
Hos cot cuftodiebat fep uicecomes de Middelfexe
Wills camerari redd uicecomiti regis p annu
vI . fol . p terra ubi fedet uinea fua.

MIDDLESEX

LIST OF LANDHOLDERS IN MIDDLESEX   126 d

1 King William
2 The Archbishop of Canterbury
3 The Bishop of London and
   his Canons
4 Westminster Abbey
5 Holy Trinity Abbey, Rouen
6 Barking Abbey
7 Earl Roger
8 The Count of Mortain
9 Geoffrey de Mandeville
10 Arnulf of Hesdin
11 Walter son of Othere
12 Walter of St. Valery

13 Richard son of Count Gilbert
14 Robert Gernon
15 Robert Fafiton
16 Robert son of Rozelin
17 Robert Blunt
18 Roger of Raismes
19 William son of Ansculf
20 Edward of Salisbury
21 Aubrey de Vere
22 Ranulf brother of Ilger
23 Derman [of London]
24 Countess Judith
and [25] The King's Almsmen

---

[1]   **[LAND OF THE KING]**   127 a

In OSSULSTONE* Hundred

1 King William holds 12½ acres of NOMANSLAND.
The value of this land was and is 5s.
   King Edward held it similarly.

2 In the same Hundred the King has 30 cottagers who pay
14s 10½d a year.

3 At HOLBORN the King has 2 cottagers who pay 20d a year
to the King's Sheriff. Before 1066 the Sheriff of Middlesex
always had charge of them.

4 William the Chamberlain pays the King's Sheriff 6s a year
for the land on which his vineyard stands.

Archieps Lanfranc tenet *HESA*

.p. LVIIII. hidis. Tra. e. XL. carucar. Ad dñiu ptiñ

.XII. hide.7 ibi funt. II. carucæ. Int franc 7 uiłłos.

funt. XXVI. car.7 adhuc XII. poffent. ee.

Ibi pbr hĩ. I. hid.7 III. milites. VI. hid 7 dim.7 I:. uiłłi

II. hid.7 XII. uiłłi qfq dimid hidā.7 XX. uiłłi. qfq

.I. uirg tre.7 XL. uiłłi. qfq dim uirg.7 XVI. bord

de. II. hid. ĩbi funt. XII. cot.7 II. ferui. Ibi. I. moliñ

IIII. fol.7 ptū.I.c.   Paftura ad pecuniā

uillæ. Silua. CCCC. porc.7 III. folid.

In totis ualentijs ualet. XXX. lib.7 qdo recep. XII. lib.

T.R.E. XL. lib. Hoc Maneriū tenuit Stigand arcħ.

In *HVND* de Gara. tenet. L. archieps *HERGES*.

Pro. c. hid fe defendeb T.R.E.7 m facit. Tra. e. LXX.

car. Ad dñiu ptiñ. XXX. hide.7 ibi fuŋ. IIII. carucæ.

7 V. pot fieri. Int franc 7 uiłł. XLV. car.7 XVI.

plus poss. ee. Ibi pbr. I. hidā.7 III. milites. VI. hid

7 fub eis maneŋ. VII. hoes. Ibi. XIII. uiłłi qfq dim

hid.7 XXVIII. uiłłi qfq de. I. uirg.7 XLVIII. uiłł

qfq dim uirg.7 XIII. uiłł de. IIII. hid.7 II. cot de

XIII. acris.7 II. ferui. Pafta ad pecun uillæ. Silua

ĩĩ. mił porc. In totis ualentijs ual. LVI. lib.

7 qdo recep. XX. lib. T.R.E. LX. lib. Hoc Maner

ten Leuuin die qua rex. E. fuit uiuus 7 mortuus.

2   LAND OF THE ARCHBISHOP OF CANTERBURY

[In the Hundred of ELTHORNE]

1 Archbishop Lanfranc holds HAYES for 59 hides. Land for
40 ploughs. 12 hides belong to the lordship; 2 ploughs there.
There are 26 ploughs between the Frenchmen* and the
villagers; a further 12 possible.
   A priest has 1 hide; 3 men-at-arms, 6½ hides;
    2 villagers, 2 hides; 12 villagers, ½ hide each;
    20 villagers, 1 virgate of land each; 40 villagers,
    ½ virgate each; 16 smallholders with 2 hides;
    12 cottagers; 2 slaves.
   1 mill, 4s; meadow for 1 plough*; pasture for the
    village livestock; woodland, 400 pigs*, and 3s too.
Total value £30; when acquired £12; before 1066 £40.
Archbishop Stigand held this manor.

In the Hundred of GORE

2 Archbishop Lanfranc holds HARROW. It answered for
100 hides before 1066, and does so now. Land for 70
ploughs. 30 hides belong to the lordship; 4 ploughs there;
5 (more)* possible. 45 ploughs between the Frenchmen and
the villagers; 16 more possible.
   A priest, 1 hide; 3 men-at- arms, 6 hides, and under
    them dwell 7 men; 13 villagers with ½ hide each;
    28 villagers with 1 virgate each; 48 villagers with ½
    virgate each; 13 villagers with 4 hides; 2 cottagers
    with 13 acres; 2 slaves.
   Pasture for the village livestock; woodland, 2000 pigs.
Total value £56; when acquired £20; before 1066 £60.
Earl Leofwin held this manor in 1066.

In *Hvnd* de Heletorne . tenet Goisfrid de man

neuilla . ii . hid de Arch . L . Tra . i . car .7 ibi eſt . i .

uills cũ . i . car q̃ ten trã .7 iiii . cot . Silua . xx . porc.

H tra ualet xii . ſol .7 qdo recep̃ . ſimilit . T.R.E.

xiiii . ſol . Hanc tenuit Turbert hõ com̃ Leuuini.

ñ potuit mittere ext̃ Herges M̃ archiep̃i.

.iii. TERRA EP̃I LVNDONIENSIS.

In Oſulueſtan *Hvnd* .tenet ep̃s Lundonienſis

STIBENHEDE . xxx.ii . hid . Tra . ẽ . xxv . car . Ad

dñiũ p̃tin xiiii . hidæ .7 ibi ſunt . iii . car .7 uilloʒ xx.ii.

car . Ibi . xliiii . uilti . q̃ſq̃ de . i . uirg .7 vii . uilti . q̃ſq̃

de dim̃ hida .7 ix . uilti q̃ſq̃ de dim̃ uirg .7 xlvi . cot

de . i . hida . reddt p ann̄ . xxx . ſolid . Ibi . iiii . molini

de . iiii . liɓ 7 xvi . ſol . iiii . den min̄ . P̃tũ . xxv . car.

Paſta ad pecun̄ uillæ .7 xv . ſolid . Silua q̃ngent porc.

7 xl . ſol . In totis ualentijs ualet xlviii . liɓ .7 qdo

recep̃ ſimilit . T.R.E. l . liɓ . Hoc M̃ fuit 7 ẽ de ep̃atu.

In ead uilla tenet Hugo de berneres ſub ep̃o . v . hid

7 i . virg træ . Tra . ẽ . iiii . car . In dñio . i . car .7 uilti . iii . car̃.

Ibi . i . uilt de dim̃ hida .7 vi . uilti de . iii . uirg .7 ii . bord

de dim̃ uirg .7 iii . cot de . ii . acris 7 dim̃ .7 i . molin̄

de . lx.vi . ſol 7 viii . den̄ . P̃tũ . iiii . car̃ . Silua . cl . porc.

7 iii . ſol 7 dim̃ . Int totũ ualet . vi . liɓ . qdo recep̃ ſimi

liter . T.R.E. vii . liɓ . De hoc M̃ ten Sired . ii . hid 7 dim̃.

canonic fuit S̃ Pauli . potuit dare 7 uendere cui uoluit

3 Geoffrey de Mandeville holds 2 hides from Archbishop
   Lanfranc. Land for 1 plough.
       1 villager with 1 plough, who holds the land; 4 cottagers.
       Woodland, 20 pigs.
   Value of this land, 12s; when acquired the same;
   before 1066, 14s.
       Thorbert, Earl Leofwin's man, held it; he could not put it,
   or sell it, outside the Archbishop's manor of Harrow.

3   **LAND OF THE BISHOP OF LONDON**

In OSSULSTONE Hundred

1 The Bishop of London holds STEPNEY. 32 hides. Land for
   25 ploughs. 14 hides belong to the lordship; 3 ploughs
   there. 22 villagers' ploughs.
       44 villagers with 1 virgate each; 7 villagers with
       ½ hide each; 9 villagers with ½ virgate each;
       46 cottagers with 1 hide pay 30s a year.
       4 mills at £4 16s less 4d; meadow for 25 ploughs;
       pasture for the village livestock, and 15s too;
       woodland, 500 pigs and 40s too.
   Total value £48; when acquired the same; before 1066 £50.
   This manor was and is the Bishopric's.

In the same village*

2 Hugh of Bernieres holds 5 hides and 1 virgate of land
   under the Bishop. Land for 4 ploughs. In lordship 1
   plough. The villagers, 3 ploughs.
       1 villager with ½ hide; 6 villagers with 3 virgates;
       2 smallholders with ½ virgate; 3 cottagers with 2½ acres.
       1 mill at 66s 8d; meadow for 4 ploughs; woodland,
       150 pigs, and 3½s too.
   Total value £6; when acquired the same; before 1066 £7.
       Sired held 2½ hides of this manor; he was a Canon of

absq̞ Licentia epi.T.R.E.Canonici S̄ Pauli tenuer̄

II.hiđ 7 dim̄.de dn̄ico uictu suo.7 Doding ten⁹.I.uirḡ

7 I.molin̄ de ꝑpo manerio epi.n̄ potuit dare uel uen

dere ꝑter ej licentiā.

In ead uilla tenet uxor Brien.v.hiđ de epo.T̄ra.ē

II.car̄ 7 dim̄.In dn̄io.ē.I.car̄.7 I.car̄ potest fieri uill̄.

Ibi.I.uill̄ de dim̄ hida.redđ ꝑ ann̄.IIII.sol̄ de domo

sua.7 alt uill̄ de dim̄ hida.redđ.VIII.sol̄.Rogeri uicecom̄⁹

ten̄ dim̄ hiđ.7 xv.borđ de.x.acris.redđ.IX.solid̄.

Silua.LX.porc̄.Pasta ad pecun̄ uillæ.7 v.solid̄.Int̄

totū ualet.LX.sol̄.qdo recep̄ similit̄.T.R.E.c.solid̄.

Hanc tr̄a ten̄ Will̄s ep̄s in dn̄io.die q̄ rex.E.fuit uiuus

7 mortuus.in M̄ de Stibenhede.

In ead uilla tenet Rannulf̄ flābard⁹ de epo.III.hiđ 7 dimiđ.

127 c T̄ra.ē.v.car̄.Ibi in dn̄io.II.car̄.7 III.car̄ uill̄.

Ibi.XIIII.borđ.de.I.hiđ 7 dim̄.P̄tū.II.car̄.7 II.solid̄.

Pasta n̄.ē.Nem̄⁹ ad sepes faciend̄.Int totū ualet.IIII.

lib̄.qdo recep̄ similit̄.T.R.E.c.sol̄.Hanc tr̄a tenuit

Goduin sub epo.Will̄o.n̄ potuit dare ul̄ uendere

absq̞ licentia epi.T.R.E.

In ead uilla tenet Will̄s de uer de epo.I.hidā.T̄ra.

ē.I.car̄.7 ibi ē in dn̄io.H̄ tra ual̄.xvI.sol̄.qdo recep̄

similit̄.T.R.E.xx.sol̄.Hanc tr̄a tenuit Will̄s in dn̄io

cū suo M̄ Stibenhede.T.R.E.

In ead uilla tenet Engelbric canonic⁹ de epo.I.hidā

7 I.uirḡ.T̄ra.ē.I.car̄.7 ibi.ē in dn̄io.Ibi.I.uill̄s de.I.

uirḡ.7 IIII.borđ quisq̞ de.vII.acs.7 I.cot.Int totū

ualet xL.sol̄.qdo recep̄ simil̄.T.R.E.L.sol̄.Isđe canon̄

tenuit de epo.W.T.R.E.n̄ potuit uende.

St. Paul's; he could grant or sell to whom he would
without the Bishop's permission before 1066*.
  The Canons of St. Paul's held 2½ hides for their
household supplies.
  Doding held 1 virgate and 1 mill of the Bishop's own
manor; he could not grant or sell except with his permission.

3 Brian's wife holds 5 hides from the Bishop. Land for 2½
ploughs. In lordship 1 plough. 1 plough possible for the
villagers.
    1 villager with ½ hide pays 4s a year on his house; another
    villager with ½ hide pays 8s; Roger the Sheriff holds
    ½ hide; 15 smallholders with 10 acres pay 9s.
  Woodland, 60 pigs; pasture for the village livestock, and 5s too.
In total, value 60s; when acquired the same; before 1066, 100s.
  Bishop William held this land in lordship in the manor
of Stepney in 1066.

4 Ranulf Flambard holds 3½ hides from the Bishop.
Land for 5 ploughs. In lordship 2 ploughs. 3 villagers' ploughs.   127 c
  14 smallholders with 1½ hides.
    Meadow for 2 ploughs, and 2s too; no pasture; wood
    for making fences.
In total, value £4; when acquired the same; before 1066, 100s.
  Godwin held this land under Bishop William; he could
not grant or sell it without the Bishop's permission before 1066.

5 William de Vere holds 1 hide from the Bishop. Land for
1 plough; it is there, in lordship.
Value of this land, 16s; when acquired the same; before 1066, 20s.
  Bishop William held this land in lordship with his manor
of Stepney before 1066.

6 Canon Engelbert holds 1 hide and 1 virgate from the Bishop.
  Land for 1 plough; it is there, in lordship.
    1 villager with 1 virgate; 4 smallholders with 7 acres each;
    1 cottager.
In total, value 40s; when acquired the same; before 1066, 50s.
  The Canon also held it from Bishop William before 1066;
he could not sell.

In ead uilla tenet eps̄ Lisiacensis de epō Lundoniensi
.i. hid 7 dimid. Tra.ē.i. car̄.7 dim car̄ ē ibi.7 dimid
potest fieri. Ibi.ii.borđ đsq̄ de.v.acs.7 ii.cot de.iiii.
acs.7 i.cot. Int tot̄ ualet.xl.sot̄.qdo recep̄ similit̄.
T.R.E.'L.sot̄.Hanc tr̄a tenuit Wilt̄s eps̄ in dn̄io.die qua
rex.E.fuit uiuus 7 mortuus.
In ead uilla tenet Wilt̄s camer' de epō.i.hiđ 7 dim.7 i.uirg.
Tra.ē.i.car̄ 7 dim. Ibi in dn̄io.i.car̄.7 dim potest fieri.
Ibi.i.uilt̄ de.i.uirg.7 vi.borđ de.v.acs. Int tot̄u
ualet.xxx.sot̄.qdo recep̄ similit̄.T.R.E.'xl.sot̄.Hanc
tra tenuit.W.eps̄ in dn̄io.die qua rex.E.obijt.
In ead tenet Aluric chacepul 9 de epō.i.hiđ.Tra.ē.i.car̄.sed
car̄ deest.H̄ tra uat̄.x.sot̄.qdo recep̄ simit̄.T.R.E.'xiii.
sot̄ 7 iiii.den̄.Hanc tra tenuit eps̄ Wilt̄s in dn̄io.T.R.E.
In ead uilla tenet Edmund f.Algot' 9 de epō.i.molin̄.qđ ualet
xxxii.sot̄ 7 vi.den̄.qdo recep̄ similit̄.s̄q n̄ fuit ibi.T.R.E.
In ead uilla tenet Aluuin f.Britmar 9.i.molin̄ qđ ualet.xx.sot̄.
qdo recep̄ simit̄.T.R.E.similit̄.Ipsemet ten̄ de.W.epō.
₃ In FVLEHAM.tenet eps̄ Lundoniæ.xl.hidas.
Tra.ē.xl.caruc̄.Ad dn̄ium ptin̄.xiii.hidæ.7|iiii.car̄. Ibi sunt
Int̄ franc̄ 7 uilt̄.xxvi.car̄.7 x.plus poss̄ fieri. Ibi
v.uilt̄i đsq̄.i.hidā.7 xiii.uilt̄i quisq̄ de.i.uirg.
7 xxxiiii.uilt̄.đsq̄ dim uirg.7 xxii.cot de dim hida.
7 viii.cot de suis hortis.Int francigen̄ 7 đsdā burḡ
Lundon̄.xxiii.hiđ đe tra uilt̄oz̄.Sub eis maneꝗ int̄
uilt̄os 7 borđ.xxx un.P̄tū.xl.car̄.Pasta ad pecun̄
uillæ.De dimiđ gurgite.x.sot̄.Silua mille porc̄.
7 xvii.den̄.In totis ualentijs ualet.xl.lib̄.qdo recep̄
similit̄.T.R.E.'L.lib̄.Hoc ₃ fuit & est de episcopatu.

7   The Bishop of Lisieux* holds 1½ hides from the Bishop of
    London. Land for 1 plough; ½ plough there; ½ possible.
       2 smallholders with 5 acres each; 2 cottagers with
          4 acres; 1 cottager.
    In total, value 40s; when acquired the same; before 1066, 50s.
       Bishop William held this land in lordship in 1066.

8   William the Chamberlain holds 1½ hides and 1 virgate from the
    Bishop. Land for 1½ ploughs. In lordship 1 plough; ½ possible.
       1 villager with 1 virgate; 6 smallholders with 5 acres.
    In total, value 30s; when acquired the same; before 1066, 40s.
       Bishop William held this land in lordship in 1066.

9   Aelfric Catchpoll holds 1 hide from the Bishop. Land for 1 plough;
    but the plough is not there.
    Value of this land, 10s; when acquired the same; before 1066, 13s 4d.
       Bishop William held this land in lordship in 1066.

10 Edmund son of Algot holds 1 mill from the Bishop.
    Value 32s 6d; when acquired the same; but it was not there
    before 1066.

11 Alwin son of Brictmer holds 1 mill.
    Value 20s; when acquired the same; before 1066 the same.
    He held it himself from Bishop William.

12 M. In FULHAM the Bishop of London holds 40 hides. Land for
    40 ploughs. 13 hides belong to the lordship; 4 ploughs there.
    26 ploughs between the Frenchmen and the villagers; 10 more
    possible.
       5 villagers, 1 hide each; 13 villagers with 1 virgate each;
          34 villagers, ½ virgate each; 22 cottagers with ½ hide;
          8 cottagers with their gardens. Between the Frenchmen and
          some London burgesses, 23 hides of villagers' land; under
          them dwell 31 of the villagers and smallholders.
       Meadow for 40 ploughs; pasture for the village livestock;
          from half a weir, 10s; woodland, 1000 pigs, and 17d too.
    Total value £40; when acquired the same; before 1066 £50.
       This manor is and was the Bishopric's.

In ead uilla.tenet Fulchered de epo Londoniæ.v.hid. Tra.ē.iii.car.In dñio.i.car.7 i.car uitto̴.7 tcia poffet fieri.Ibi.vi.uitti de dim hida.7 iiii.cot de viii. acris.7 iii.cot.p̃tu.i.bou.Pafta ad pecuñ uillæ. Silua.ccc.porc.In totis ualentijs uat.lx.fot.qdo recep̃.fimilit.T.R.E.c.fot.Hanc trā tenuer.ii.fochi. hões epi London fuer.ñ potuer dare uel uende abfq̴ licentia epi.T.R.E.

☧ In ead uilla teney canonici S Pauli de rege.v.hid. p uno Man.Tra.ē.v.car.Ad dñiu ptiñ.iii.hide. 7 ibi funt.ii.car.Vitti.ii.car.7 tcia pot fieri.Ibi.viii. uitti.qfq̴ de.i.uirg.7 vii.uitti.qfq̴ de dim uirg. 7 vii.bord.qfq̴ de.v.acs.7 xvi.cot.7 ii.ferui.p̃tu v.car.Pafta ad pecuñ uille.Silua.c.l.porc.Int totu uat.viii.lib.qdo recep̃ fimilit.T.R.E: x.lib.Hoc ☧ tenuer ide canonici S Pauli in dñio.T.R.E.7 ē de uictu eo̴.

IN OSVLVESTANE HVND.

In TVEVERDE tenet Durand canonic S Pauli de rege ii.h træ.Tra.ē.i.car 7 dim.Ibi funt.iii.uitti de dim hida.7 dim uirg.Pafta ad pecuñ uille.Silua.c.porc. H tra ualet.xxx.fot.qdo recep̃ fimilit.T.R.E.xx.fot. In ead uilla tenet Gueri canonic S Pauli.ii.h træ. Tra.ē.i.car 7 dim.In dñio.ē car.7 dim poteft fieri. Ibi.ii.uitt de.i.uirg.7 i.bord de.vi.acs.7 iii.cot. Silua.l.porc.H tra ualet xxx.fot.qdo recep̃. fimilit.T.R.E.xx.fot.Hoc ☧ jacuit 7 jacet in æccta S Pauli.in dñio canonico̴.

13 In the same village Fulcred holds 5 hides from the Bishop of   127 d
London. Land for 3 ploughs. In lordship 1 plough. 1 villagers'
plough; a third possible.
    6 villagers with ½ hide; 4 cottagers with 8 acres; 3 cottagers.
    Meadow for 1 ox; pasture for the village livestock; woodland,
      300 pigs.
Total value 60s; when acquired the same; before 1066, 100s.
    Two Freemen held this land before 1066; they were the Bishop
of London's men; they could not grant or sell without the
Bishop's permission.

14 M. In the same village the Canons of St. Paul's hold 5 hides from
the King as one manor. Land for 5 ploughs. 3 hides belong to
the lordship; 2 ploughs there. The villagers, 2 ploughs; a third
possible.
    8 villagers with 1 virgate each; 7 villagers with ½ virgate
    each; 7 smallholders with 5 acres each; 16 cottagers; 2 slaves.
    Meadow for 5 ploughs; pasture for the village livestock;
    woodland, 150 pigs.
In total, value £8; when acquired the same; before 1066, £10.
    Before 1066 the Canons of St. Paul's held this manor in
lordship; it is for their supplies.

   [also] in OSSULSTONE Hundred*
15 In TWYFORD Durand, a Canon of St. Paul's, holds 2 hides of land
from the King. Land for 1½ ploughs.
    3 villagers with ½ hide and ½ virgate.
    Pasture for the village livestock; woodland, 100 pigs.
Value of this land 30s; when acquired the same; before 1066, 20s.

16 In the same village Gyrth, a Canon of St. Paul's, holds 2 hides of
land. Land for 1½ ploughs. In lordship 1 plough; ½ possible.
    2 villagers with 1 virgate; 1 smallholder with 6 acres; 3 cottagers.
    Woodland, 50 pigs.
Value of this land 30s; when acquired the same; before 1066, 20s.
    This manor lay and lies in (the lands of) St. Paul's Church, in
the lordship of the Canons.

WELLESDONE tenent canonici S̃ Pauli . p̄ xv.

hid̃ ſe defendebat ſēp . T̃ra . ē . xv . car̃ . Ibi uiłłi.

viii . car̃ . 7 vii . poſſ fieri . Ibi . xxv . uiłłi . 7 v . bord̃.

Silua q̃ngent porc̃ . In totis ualentijs ualet . vi . lib̃.

7 vi . ſol̃ . 7 vi . den̄ . q̃do recep̄ . ſimilit̃ . T.R.E.⁖ xii . lib̃.

Hoc m̃ teneñ uiłłi ad firmā canonicoᷓ . In dñio

nil habet̃ . H̃ maner̃ fuit de dñico uiᷓtu . T.R.E.

HERVLVESTVNE teneñ canonici p . i . m̃ d̃|e ᵖʳᵒ v . hid̃ ſe defd̃.

T̃ra . ē . iiii . car̃ . In dñio . ii . car̃ . 7 uiłł dim̃ car̃ . Vna

car̃ 7 dim̃ poteſt fieri . Ibi . xii . uiłłi . q̃ſq̃ de . i . uirg̃.

7 x . uiłłi q̃ſq̃ de dim̃ uirga . Silua . c . porc̃ . Int totū

ualet . xxx.v . ſolid̃ . q̃do recep̄ . ſimilit̃ . T.R.E.⁖ iiii . lib̃.

Hoc m̃ fuit T.R.E. 7 m̃ in dñio canonicoᷓ S̃ Pauli.

Rugemere tenet Radulf⁹ canonic⁹ p . ii . hid̃ .| ſe defend̃⸱ T̃ra

ē . i . car̃ 7 dim̃ . Ibi in dñio . i . car̃ . 7 dim̃ car̃ poteſt

fieri . Nem ad ſepes . 7 iiii . ſol̃ . H̃ tra ual̃ xxxv . ſol̃.

q̃do recep̄ ſimilit̃ . T.R.E.⁖ xl . ſol̃ . T.R.E. fuit 7 m̃ eſt

ʄin dñio canon̄.

128 a m̃ *TOTEHELE* tenent canonici S̃ Pauli . p . v . hid̃ ſe

defendebat ſēp . T̃ra . ē . iiii . car̃ . Ibi ſunt . iii . car̃

7 dimid̃ . 7 adhuc dim̃ poteſt fieri . Ibi . iiii . uiłł 7 iiii⸱

bord̃ . Silua . cl . porc̃ . 7 xx . ſol̃ de Herbagia.

In totis ualentijs ualet . iiii . lib̃ . q̃do recep̄⸴ ſimilit̃.

T.R.E.⁖ c . ſol̃ . Hoc m̃ jacuit 7 jacet in dñio S̃ Pauli.

m̃ Ad Sᷓm Pancratiū tenent canonici S̃ Pauli . iiii ᵒʳ.

hid̃ . T̃ra . ē . ii . car̃ . Viłłi hñt . i . car̃ . 7 alia car̃ poteſt

fieri . Nem ad ſepes . Paſta ad pecun̄ . 7 xx . den̄ . Ibi

iiii . uiłłi q̃ teneñ hanc t̃ra ſub canon̄ . 7 vii . cot̃.

In totis ualentijs . ual̃ . xl . ſol̃ . q̃do recep̄ ſimilit̃.

T.R.E.⁖ lx . ſol̃ . Hoc m̃ fuit 7 eſt in dñio S̃ Pauli.

17   The Canons of St. Paul's hold WILLESDEN. It always answered for 15
      hides. Land for 15 ploughs. The villagers, 8 ploughs; 7 possible.
          25 villagers; 5 smallholders.
          Woodland, 500 pigs.
      Total value £6 6s 6d; when acquired the same; before 1066 £12.
          The villagers hold this manor for the Canons' revenue. Nothing
      is held in lordship; the manor was for their household supplies
      before 1066.

18   The Canons hold HARLESDEN as one manor*. It answers* for 5 hides.
      Land for 4 ploughs. In lordship 2 ploughs. The villagers, ½
      plough; 1½ ploughs possible.
          12 villagers with 1 virgate each; 10 villagers with ½ virgate each.
          Woodland, 100 pigs.
      In total, value 35s; when acquired the same; before 1066 £4.
          This manor was in the lordship of the Canons of St. Paul's
      before 1066 and still is.

19   Canon Ralph holds RUG MOOR*. It answers for 2 hides. Land for 1½
      ploughs. In lordship 1 plough; ½ plough possible.
          Wood for fences, and 4s too.
      Value of this land, 35s; when acquired the same; before 1066, 40s.
          Before 1066 it was in the Canons' lordship and still is.

20 M. The Canons of St. Paul's hold TOTTENHAM (COURT). It always   128 a
       answered for 5 hides. Land for 4 ploughs. 3½ ploughs there;
      a further ½ possible.
          4 villagers; 4 smallholders.
          Woodland, 150 pigs; from grazing, 20s.
      Total value £4; when acquired the same; before 1066, 100s.
          This manor lay and lies in the lordship of St. Paul's.

21 M. At ST. PANCRAS the Canons of St. Paul's hold 4 hides. Land for 2
       ploughs. The villagers have 1 plough; another plough possible.
          Wood for fences; pasture for the livestock, and 20d too.
          4 villagers, who hold this land under the Canons; 7 cottagers.
      Total value 40s; when acquired the same; before 1066, 60s.
          This manor was and is in the lordship of St. Paul's.

In Isendone hn̄t canon̄ S̄ Pauli . ɪɪ . hid . T̄ra . ɪ . car̄

7 dim̄ . Ibi . ē . ɪ . car̄ . 7 dim̄ poteſt fieri . Ibi . ɪɪɪ . uiłłi

de . ɪ . uirḡ . Paſt̄a ad pecun̄ uiłł . H̄ tra uał 7 ualuit

xʟ . ſoł . H̄ jacuit 7 jacet in dn̄io æccłæ S̄ Pauli .

In ead uilla hn̄t ipſi canon̄ . ɪɪ . h̄ t̄ . . Ad . ɪɪ . car̄

7 dim̄ ē tra ibi . 7 m̊ ſunt . Ibi . ɪɪɪɪ . uiłłi q̄ teneɴ ſub

canon̄ hanc tr̄a . 7 ɪɪɪɪ . bord̄ 7 xɪɪɪ . cot̄ . H̄ tra ualet

xxx . ſoł . q̄do recep̄ . ſimilit̄ . T.R.E. xʟ . ſoł . Hæc

jacuit 7 jacet in dn̄io æccłæ S̄ Pauli .

In Neutone hn̄t canonici S̄ Pauli . ɪɪ . hid . Ad . ɪɪ .

car̄ 7 dim̄ eſt ibi tr̄a . 7 m̊ ſunt . Ibi . ɪɪɪɪ . uiłłi . 7 xxxvɪɪ .

cot̄ de . x . acr̄ . H̄ tra uał xʟ . ɪ . ſoł . q̄do recep̄ ſimilit̄ .

T.R.E. xʟ . ſoł . Hæc jacuit 7 jacet in dn̄io S̄ Pauli .

In Hocheſtone hn̄t canon̄ S̄ Pauli . ɪ . hid̄ . T̄ra . ɪ . car̄ .

7 m̊ ibi eſt . 7 ɪɪɪ . uiłłi tenent̄ hanc tr̄a ſub canonicis .

Paſt̄a ad pecun̄ . H̄ tra ualuit 7 ualet . xx . ſoł . Hæc

jacuit 7 jacet in dn̄io æccłæ S̄ Pauli .

M̄ Hocheſtone . teneɴ canon̄ p̄ . ɪɪɪ . hid . Ad . ɪɪɪ .

car̄ eſt tr̄a . 7 ibi ſunt . 7 vɪɪ . uiłłi q̄ ten̄ hanc tr̄a .

7 xvɪ . cot̄ . Int totū ualet . ʟv . ſoł . q̄do recep̄ .

ſimilit̄ . T.R.E. ʟx . ſoł . Hoc M̄ jacuit 7 jacet

in æccła S̄ Pauli .

Canonici S̄ Pauli hn̄t ad portā epi . x . cot̄

de . ɪx . acr̄ . q̄ redd̄t p annū . xvɪɪɪ . ſoł 7 vɪ . den̄ .

T.R.E. ſimilit̄ tenuer̄ . 7 tn̄td habuer̄ .

In Staneſtaple hn̄t canon̄ . ɪɪɪɪ . hid . T̄ra . ē ad

ɪɪ . car̄ . 7 ibi ſunt m̊ . 7 vɪɪ . uiłłi q̄ ten̄ hanc tr̄a

ſub canon̄ . 7 ɪɪ . cot̄ . Paſt̄a ad pecun̄ uillæ .

22   In ISLINGTON the Canons of St. Paul's have 2 hides. Land
for 1½ ploughs. 1 plough there; ½ possible.
    3 villagers with 1 virgate.
    Pasture for the village livestock.
The value of this land is and was 40s.
It lay and lies in the lordship of St. Paul's Church.

23   In the same village the Canons themselves have 2 hides of land.
The land is for 2½ ploughs; they are there now.
    4 villagers, who hold this land under the Canons;
      4 smallholders; 13 cottagers.
Value of this land, 30s; when acquired the same; before 1066, 40s.
It lay and lies in the lordship of St. Paul's Church.

24   In (STOKE) NEWINGTON the Canons of St. Paul's have 2 hides.
The land is for 2½ ploughs; they are there now.
    4 villagers; 37 cottagers with 10 acres.
Value of this land, 41s; when acquired the same; before 1066, 40s.
It lay and lies in the lordship of St. Paul's Church.

25   In HOXTON the Canons of St. Paul's have 1 hide. Land
for 1 plough; it is there now.
    3 villagers hold this land under the Canons.
    Pasture for the livestock.
The value of this land was and is 20s.
It lay and lies in the lordship of St. Paul's Church.

26 M. The Canons hold HOXTON as 3 hides. The land is for 3 ploughs;
they are there.
    7 villagers, who hold this land; 16 cottagers.
In total, value 55s; when acquired the same; before 1066, 60s.
This manor lay and lies in (the lands of) St. Paul's Church.

27   At BISHOPSGATE the Canons of St. Paul's have 10 cottagers with 9
acres who pay 18s 6d a year. Before 1066 they held similarly
and had as much.

28   In *STANESTAPLE* the Canons have 4 hides. The land is for 2 ploughs;
they are there now.
    7 villagers, who hold this land under the Canons; 2 cottagers.
    Pasture for the village livestock; woodland, 150 pigs, and 10s too.

Silua . CL . porc . 7 x . ſol . In totis ualentijs
ual . L . ſol . qdo recep̄ ſimilit . T.R.E. ⁄ LX . ſol.
H̄ tra jacuit 7 jacet in æccła S̄ Pauli.

A̋d S̄cm Pancratiū tenet Walter canonic

128 b   S̄ Pauli . I . hid . Tra . I . car . Ibi . ē car . 7 XXIIII . hōes
qui redduꝗ . XXX . ſol p annū . H̄ tra jacuit 7 jacet
in dn̄io æccłæ S̄ Pauli.

Ⓜ *DRAITONE* teneꝗ canon S̄ Pauli . ꝓ . x . hid ſe sēp
defend . Tra ad . VI . car . Ad dn̄iū ptin̄ . v . hid . 7 I . car
ibi . ē . Viłłi hn̄t . v . car . Ibi . VIII . uiłłi de . II . hid.
7 VI . bord de xxx . ac . 7 II . cot de . IIII . ac . 7 I . bord
de . v . acr . Ibi . I . molin de XIII . ſol 7 v . den . P̊tū.
. I . car . Paſta ad pec uille . De . I . gurgite . XXXII . den.
In totis ualent ual . VI . liƀ . Qdo recep̄ ſimilit . T.R.E.
VIII . liƀ . Hoc Ⓜ jacuit 7 jacet in dn̄io æccłæ S̄ Pauli.

.IIII.   TERRA S̄CI PETRI WESTMON IN OSVLVESTANE H̄D.

Ⓜ I̋n Villa ubi ſedet æccła S̄ PETRI . tenet abƀ ejđe
loci . XIII . hid 7 dim . Tra . ē ad XI . car . Ad dn̄ium
ptin̄ . IX . hidæ 7 I . uirg . 7 ibi ſuꝗ . IIII . car . Viłłi hn̄t . VI.
car . 7 I . car plus pot fieri . Ibi . IX . uiłłi ꝗ́ſꝗ de . I . uirg.
7 I . uiłłs de . I . hida . 7 IX . uiłłi ꝗ́ſꝗ de dim uirg . 7 I . cot
de . v . ac . 7 XL . I . cot ꝗ́ reddt p ann̄ . XL . ſol ꝓ ortis ſuis.
P̊tū . XI . car . Paſta ad pecun uillæ . Silua . c porc.
7 XXV . dom militū abƀis 7 alioꝣ hōum . qui reddt
VIII . ſol p annū . In totis ualent ual . x . liƀ . Qdo
recep̄ . ſimilit . T.R.E. ⁄ XII . liƀ . Hoc Ⓜ fuit 7 eſt
in dn̄io æccłæ S̄ PETRI . Weſtmonaſterij.

Total value 50s; when acquired the same; before 1066, 60s.
This land lay and lies in (the lands of) St. Paul's Church.

29   At ST. PANCRAS Walter, a Canon of St. Paul's, holds 1 hide.   128 b
Land for 1 plough. The plough is there.
   24 men, who pay 30s a year.
This land lay and lies in the lordship of St. Paul's Church.

[In ELTHORNE Hundred] *
30 M. The Canons of St. Paul's hold (WEST) DRAYTON*. It always answered
for 10 hides. Land for 6 ploughs. 5 hides belong to the
lordship; 1 plough there. The villagers have 5 ploughs.
   8 villagers with 2 hides; 6 smallholders with 30 acres;
   2 cottagers with 4 acres; 1 smallholder with 5 acres.
   1 mill at 13s 5d; meadow for 1 plough; pasture for the village
   livestock; from 1 weir, 32d.
Total value £6; when acquired the same; before 1066 £8.
This manor lay and lies in the lordship of St. Paul's Church.

4   LAND OF ST. PETER'S OF WESTMINSTER

In OSSULSTONE Hundred
1 M. In the village where St. Peter's Church stands the Abbot of that
monastery holds 13½ hides. The land is for 11 ploughs. 9 hides
and 1 virgate belong to the lordship; 4 ploughs there. The
villagers have 6 ploughs; 1 more plough possible.
   9 villagers with 1 virgate each; 1 villager with 1 hide;
   9 villagers with ½ virgate each; 1 cottager with 5 acres;
   41 cottagers, who pay 40s a year for their gardens.
   Meadow for 11 ploughs; pasture for the village livestock;
   woodland, 100 pigs; 25 houses of the Abbot's men-at-arms
   and other men, who pay 8s a year.
Total value £10; when acquired the same; before 1066 £12.
   This manor was and is in the lordship of St. Peter's
Church, Westminster.

In ead uilla ten̄ Bainiard . iii . hid̄ de abƀe . Tra . ē
ad . ii . car̄ . 7 ibi fuɴ in dn̄io . 7 i . cot̄ . Silua . c . porc̄.
Pafta ad pecun̄ . Ibi . iiii . arpenni uineæ . nouit̄ plant̄.
In totis ualent̄ ual . lx . fot̄ . Q̣do recep̄ . xx . fot̄ . T R E.
. vi . liƀ . H̄ tra jacuit 7 jacet in æccta S̄ PETRI.

Ⓜ HAMESTEDE ten̄ abƀ S̄ PEK̄I . iiii . hid̄ . Tra . iii.
car̄ . Ad dn̄iū ptin̄ . iii . hid̄ 7 dim̄ . 7 ibi . ē . i . car̄ . Villi
hn̄t . i . car̄ . 7 alia pot̄ fieri . Ibi . i . uitt de . i . uirḡ . 7 v.
bord̄ de . i . uirḡ . 7 i . feru . Silua . c . porc̄ . Int totū
ual . l . fot̄ . Q̣do recep̄ . fimit̄ . T.R.E. c . fot̄.

In ead uilla ten̄ Rann̄ peurel fub abƀe . i . hid̄a
de tra uittoꝝ . Tra dim̄ car̄ . 7 ibi eft . H̄ tra ualuit
7 ual . v . folid . Hoc Ⓜ totū fimul jacuit 7 jacet in dn̄io
æcctæ S̄ PETRI.   IN SPELETORNE HVND.

Ⓜ STANES ten̄ abƀ S̄ PETRI ꝑ . xix . hid̄ . Tra eft
ad xxiiii . car̄ . Ad dn̄iū ptin̄ . xi . hidæ . 7 ibi funt
xiii . car̄ . Villi hn̄t . xi . car̄ . Ibi . iii . uitti . q̄fꝗ dim̄ ħ.
7 iiii . uitt de . i . ħ . 7 viii . uitti q̄fꝗ de dim̄ uirḡ.
7 xxxvi . bord̄ de . iii . ħ . 7 i . uitt de . i . uirḡ . 7 iiii . bord̄
de . xl . ac̄ . 7 x . bord̄ . q̄fꝗ . v . ac̄ . 7 v . cot̄ . q̄fꝗ de . iiii . ac̄.

7 viii . bord̄ de . i . uirḡ . 7 iii . cot̄ de . ix . ac̄.
7 xii . feiui . 7 xlvi . burḡ q̄ redd̄t ꝑ annū . xl . fot̄.
Ibi . vi . molini de . lxiiii . fot̄ . 7 i . guort de . vi . fot̄
7 viii . den̄ . 7 i . guort qd̄ nil redd̄ . Pafta ad pecun̄
uillæ . I'tū . xxiiii . car̄ . 7 xx . fot̄ de fup plus . Silua
xxx . porc̄ . 7 ii . arpenn̄ uineæ . Ad hoc Ⓜ ptineɴ
iiii . bereuu . 7 ibi fuer̄ . T.R.E. In totis ualentijs ual
xxxv . liƀ . Q̣do recep̄ . fimit̄ . T.R.E. xl . liƀ . Hoc Ⓜ
jacuit 7 jacet in dn̄io æcctæ S̄ PETRI.

2   In the same village Baynard holds 3 hides from the Abbot.
The land is for 2 ploughs; they are there, in lordship.
  1 cottager.
  Woodland, 100 pigs; pasture for the livestock;
    4 *arpents* of newly planted vines.
Total value 60s; when acquired 20s; before 1066 £6.
This land lay and lies in (the lands of) St. Peter's Church.

3 M. The Abbot of St. Peter's holds HAMPSTEAD. 4 hides. Land for 3
ploughs. 3½ hides belong to the lordship; 1 plough there.
The villagers have 1 plough; another possible.
  1 villager with 1 virgate; 5 smallholders with 1 virgate; 1 slave.
  Woodland, 100 pigs.
In total, value 50s; when acquired the same; before 1066, 100s.

4   In the same village Ranulf Peverel holds under the Abbot 1 hide
of villagers' land. Land for ½ plough; it is there.
The value of this land was and is 5s.
  The whole of this manor lay and lies in the lordship of
St. Peter's Church.

The Abbot of St. Peter's holds*
In SPELTHORNE Hundred

5 M. STAINES, for 19 hides. Land for 24 ploughs. 11 hides belong to the
lordship; 13 ploughs there. The villagers have 11 ploughs.
  3 villagers, ½ hide each; 4 villagers with 1 hide; 8 villagers
    with ½ virgate each; 36 smallholders with 3 hides; 1 villager
    with 1 virgate; 4 smallholders with 40 acres; 10 smallholders
    with 5 acres each; 5 cottagers with 4 acres each;
    8 smallholders with 1 virgate; 3 cottagers* with 9 acres;   128c
    12 slaves; 46 burgesses, who pay 40s a year.
  6 mills at 64s; 1 weir at 6s 8d; 1 weir which pays nothing;
    pasture for the village livestock; meadow for 24 ploughs, and
    20s over and above; woodland, 30 pigs; 2 *arpents* of vines.
  4 outliers belong to this manor; they were there before 1066.
Total value £35; when acquired the same; before 1066 £40.
This manor lay and lies in the lordship of St. Peter's Church.

Ⓜ *SVNEBERIE* ten abb̄ S̄ Petri.p̄ vii.hid. Tra. vi.

car̄.ē ibi. Ad dn̄iū p̄tin.iiii.ħ.7 ⒈car̄ ibi.ē. Vill̄i

hn̄t.iiii.car̄. Ibi p̄br̄ hē dim̄ uirg.7 viii.uill̄i.

q̄sq.⒈uirg.7 ii.uill̄i de.⒈uirg.7 v.bord de.⒈uirg.

7 v.cot.7 ⒈feru̇.p̄tū.vi.car̄.Pafta ad pecun̄ uillæ.

In totis ualentijs ualet.vi.lib̄.Q̄do recep̄.fimilit̄.

T.R.E.✓vii.lib̄.Hoc Ⓜ fuit 7 eſt in dn̄io æcclæ S̄ *PEꝄI*.

Ⓜ *SCEPERTONE* ten abb̄ S̄ PETꝄI p̄.viii.hid. Tra

ē ad.vii.car̄. Ad dn̄iū p̄tin.iii.ħ 7 dim̄.7 ibi eſt

.⒈car̄.uill̄i hn̄t.vi.car̄. Ibi.xvii.uill̄i q̄sq de.⒈uirg.

Pbr.xv.aċs.7 iii.cot de.ix.aċ.7 ii.cot 7 ii.ferui.

p̄tū.vii.c̄.Pafta ad pecun̄ uille.7 ⒈guort.de.vi.

Z̄7 xvi.fot. fot 7 viii.den̄.Int̄ tot̄ ual.vi.lib̄.Z̄Q̄do recep̄.fimil̄.

7 vi.den̄. T.R.E.✓vii.lib̄.Hoc Ⓜ fuit 7.ē in dn̄io æcclæ S̄ PETRI.

IN HELETORNE HVNDRET.

Ⓜ *GRENEFORDE* ten abb̄ S̄ PETRI.p̄ xi.hid 7 dim̄.

Tra.ē.vii.car̄. Ad dn̄iū p̄tin̄.v.hid.7 ⒈car̄ ibi.ē.

7 alia poteſt fieri.Vill̄i hn̄t.v.car̄. Ibi.⒈uill̄s hē

.⒈hid 7 ⒈uirg.7 iiii.uill̄i q̄sq de dim̄ hid.7 iiii.uill̄i

de.⒈hid.7 vii.bord de.⒈hid.Q̄dā franc.⒈hidā

7 ⒈uirg.7 iii.cot 7 vi.ferui.Silua.ccc.porc.Pafta

ad pecun̄ uillæ.In totis ualent̄.ual.vii.lib̄.Q̄do

recep̄.fimilit̄.T.R.E.✓x.lib̄.Hoc Ⓜ jacuit 7 jacet

in dn̄io æcclæ S̄ PETRI.

6 M. SUNBURY, for 7 hides. Land for 6 ploughs. 4 hides belong to
the lordship; 1 plough there. The villagers have 4 ploughs.
A priest has ½ virgate; 8 villagers, 1 virgate each; 2 villagers
with 1 virgate; 5 smallholders with 1 virgate; 5 cottagers;
1 slave.
Meadow for 6 ploughs; pasture for the village livestock.
Total value £6; when acquired the same; before 1066 £7.
This manor was and is in the lordship of St. Peter's Church.

7 M. SHEPPERTON, for 8 hides. The land is for 7 ploughs. 3½ hides
belong to the lordship; 1 plough there. The villagers have
6 ploughs.
17 villagers with 1 virgate each; a priest, 15 acres; 3
cottagers with 9 acres; 2 cottagers; 2 slaves.
Meadow for 7 ploughs; pasture for the village livestock;
1 weir at 6s 8d.
In total, value £6 16s 6d; when acquired the same; before 1066 £7.
This manor was and is in the lordship of St. Peter's Church.

In ELTHORNE Hundred

8 M. GREENFORD, for 11½ hides. Land for 7 ploughs. 5 hides belong to
the lordship; 1 plough there; another possible. The villagers
have 5 ploughs.
1 villager has 1 hide and 1 virgate; 4 villagers with ½ hide each;
4 villagers with 1 hide; 7 smallholders with 1 hide; a Frenchman,
1 hide and 1 virgate; 3 cottagers; 6 slaves.
Woodland, 300 pigs; pasture for the village livestock.
Total value £7; when acquired the same; before 1066 £10.
This manor lay and lies in the lordship of St. Peter's Church.

ꝳ *HANEWELLE* ten abƀ Ŝ PEꝛI . ꝑ . VIII . hiđ ſe defend.

Tra . v . caꝛ . Ad dñiũ ptiñ . IIII . ħ . 7 I . uirg . 7 I . caꝛ ibi . ē.

Viłłi hñt . IIII . caꝛ . Ibi . I . uiłłs de . II . hiđ . 7 IIII . uiłłi.

de . I . hiđ . 7 VI . borđ de . III . uirg . 7 IIII . cot . 7 II . ſerui.

Ibi . I . moliñ de . II . ſoł 7 II . den . Ƥtũ . I . caꝛ . Silua.

L . porc . In totis ualent uał . c 7 x . ſoł . Q̇do receꝑ.

ſimił . T.R.E. VII . liƀ . Hoc ꝳ fuit 7 . ē in dñio Ŝ PEꝛI.

ꝳ *COVELIE* . ten abƀ Ŝ PETRI . ꝑ . II . hiđ ſe defend

Tra . ē . I . caꝛ . Ad dñiũ ptiñ . ·I . hida 7 dim . 7 ibi . ē . I.

caꝛ . Ibi . II . uiłłi de dim ħ . 7 I . cot . Ƥtũ dim caꝛ.

128 d

Paſta ad pec uille . Silua . XL . porc . 7 moliñ . de . v . ſoł.

Ħ tra uał . XXX . ſoł . Q̇do receꝑ . ſimiłt . T.R.E. XL . ſoł.

Hanc tꝛa tenuit 7 tenet in dñio Ŝ Petr Weſtmon.

In *HVND* de Gare . ten Wiłłs camerariꝰ ſub abƀe

Ŝ PETRI . II . hiđ 7 dim in Chingeſberie . Tra . II . caꝛ.

In dñio . I . caꝛ . 7 uiłłi . I . caꝛ . Ibi . v . uiłłi . qſꝗ de . I . uirg.

7 I . cot . Silua . cc . porc . Ħ tra uał . XXX . ſoł . Q̇do receꝑ.

ſimiłt . T.R.E. LX . ſoł . Hanc tꝛa tenuit Aluuiñ horne

teigñ regis . E . in uadimonio de q̇đã hõe Ŝ PETRI.

ꝳ *HANDONE* . ten abƀ Ŝ PETRI . ꝑ xx . hiđ ſe defend.

Tra . XVI . caꝛ . Ad dñiũ ptiñ . x . hide . 7 ibi ſuɴ . III.

caꝛ . Viłłi hñt . VIII . caꝛ . 7 v adhuc poſſ fieri . Ibi

pƀr hꞇ . I . uirg . 7 III . uiłłi qſꝗ dim ħ . 7 VII . uiłłi

qſꝗ . I . uirg . 7 XVI . uiłłi . qſꝗ dim uirg . 7 XII . borđ

q̇ teneɴ dim hiđ . 7 VI . cot 7 I . ſeru . Ƥtũ . II . boũ.

Silua . mille porc . 7 x . ſoł . In totis ualent uał . VIII.

liƀ . Q̇do receꝑ . ſimiłt . T.R.E. XII . liƀ . Hoc ꝳ

jacuit 7 jacet in dñio eccłe Ŝ PETRI.

9 M. HANWELL. It answers for 8 hides. Land for 5 ploughs. 4 hides
and 1 virgate belong to the lordship; 1 plough there.
The villagers have 4 ploughs.
  1 villager with 2 hides; 4 villagers with 1 hide;
    6 smallholders with 3 virgates; 4 cottagers; 2 slaves.
  1 mill at 2s 2d; meadow for 1 plough; woodland, 50 pigs.
Total value 110s; when acquired the same; before 1066 £7.
This manor was and is in the lordship of St. Peter's.

10 M. COWLEY. It answers for 2 hides. Land for 1 plough. 1½ hides
belong to the lordship; 1 plough there.
  2 villagers with ½ hide; 1 cottager.
  Meadow for ½ plough; pasture for the village livestock;   128 d
    woodland, 40 pigs; 1 mill at 5s.
Value of this land, 30s; when acquired the same; before 1066, 40s.
St. Peter's of Westminster held and holds this land in lordship.

In the Hundred of GORE

11   William the Chamberlain holds 2½ hides in KINGSBURY under the
Abbot of St. Peter's. Land for 2 ploughs. In lordship 1 plough.
The villagers, 1 plough.
  5 villagers with 1 virgate each; 1 cottager.
  Woodland, 200 pigs.
Value of this land, 30s; when acquired the same; before 1066, 60s.
  Alwin Horne, a thane of King Edward's, held this land in pledge
from one of St. Peter's men.

12 M. The Abbot of St. Peter's holds HENDON. It answers for 20 hides.
Land for 16 ploughs. 10 hides belong to the lordship; 3 ploughs
there. The villagers have 8 ploughs; a further 5 possible.
  A priest has 1 virgate; 3 villagers, ½ hide each; 7 villagers,
    1 virgate each; 16 villagers, ½ virgate each; 12 smallholders
    who hold ½ hide; 6 cottagers; 1 slave.
  Meadow for 2 oxen; woodland, 1000 pigs, and 10s too.
Total value £8; when acquired the same; before 1066 £12.
This manor lay and lies in the lordship of St. Peter's Church.

.V. TERRA SCÆ ẜINITATIS DE MONTE ROTOM.

Ꝏ *HERMODESWORDE*.tenet abb ẜ *ẜINITATIS* ^{Rotomag'.}

de rege.ꝑ xxx.hiđ ſe defenđ.Tra.ē xx.caſ.

Ad dñiū ptin.VIII.hidæ.7 ibi ſuɴ.III.caſ.Int

franc 7 uiłłos ſuɴ.x.caſ.7 VII.adhuc poſſ.ēē.

Ibi q̇dā miles hŧ.II.hiđ.7 II.uiłłi q̇ſq̇ᷦ.I.ħ.7 II.uiłłi

de.I.ħ.7 XIIII.uiłłi q̇ſq̇ᷦ de.I.uirg.7 VI.uiłłi q̇ſq̇ᷦ de

dim uirg.7 VI.borđ q̇ſq̇ᷦ.V.ac.7 VII.cot.7 VI.ſerui.

Ibi.III.molini.de LX.ſoł.7 q̇ngent anguiłł.7 de piſcinis-

mille Anguillæ.P̄tū.xx.caſ.Paſta ad pecuɴ uillæ.

Silua q̇ngent porc.7 I.arpen uineæ.In totis ‚ualent

uał.xx.liƀ.Q̇do receꝓ.XII.liƀ.T.R.E.́xxv.liƀ.Hoc

Ꝏ tenuit coɱ Herald.7 in hoc Ꝏ fuit q̇dā ſocħs teɴ

II.hiđ de his.xxx.ħ.ɴ potuit dare ł uendē extᵃ

hermodeſworde.T.R.E.

In *SPELETORNE HVND* teɴ Hertald⁹ ɱ de rege ^{ẜ ẜinitatis}

.I.hiđ.Tra dim caſ.Ibi.ē uɴ uiłłs q̇ tenet eā.P̄tū

dim caſ.Ħ tra uał.x.ſoł.Q̇do receꝓ.ſimiliŧ.T.R.E.

ſimiliŧ.Hanc tra tenuit Goldiɴ⁹ hō comitis Heraldi.

ɴ potuit uendē ł dare ſine ej⁹ licentia.

VI. TERRA ÆCCLÆ DE BERCHINGES. *InOSVLVESTANE* HĐ.

Ꝏ *TIBVRNE* teɴ abbatiſſa de Berchinges de rege.

ꝑ.V.hiđ ſe defenđ.Tra.III.caſ.In dñio.II.hide.

7 ibi.ē.I.caſ.Viłłi hn̄t.II.caſ.Ibi.II.uiłłi de dim ħ.

7 I.uiłłs de dim uirg.7 II.borđ de.x.ac.7 III.cot.

Paſta ad pecuɴ uille.Silua.L.porc.De herbagia.

XL.den.Int totū uał.LII.ſoł.Q̇do receꝓ ſimiliŧ.T.R.E.

.c.ſoł.Hoc Ꝏ jacuit|7 jacet in æccła de Berchinges.

128 d

5   LAND OF HOLY TRINITY OF THE MOUNT, ROUEN

[In ELTHORNE Hundred]

1 M. The Abbot of Holy Trinity of Rouen holds HARMONDSWORTH from
the King. It answers for 30 hides. Land for 20 ploughs. 8 hides belong
to the lordship; 3 ploughs there. There are 10 ploughs between the
Frenchmen and the villagers; a further 7 possible.

A man-at-arms has 2 hides; 2 villagers, 1 hide each; 2 villagers
with 1 hide; 14 villagers with 1 virgate each; 6 villagers with ½
virgate each; 6 smallholders, 5 acres each; 7 cottagers; 6 slaves.

3 mills at 60s, and 500 eels; from the fishponds, 1000 eels;
meadow for 20 ploughs; pasture for the village livestock;
woodland, 500 pigs; 1 *arpent* of vines.

Total value £20; when acquired £12; before 1066 £25.

Earl Harold held this manor. In this manor there was a Freeman
who held 2 of these 30 hides; he could not grant or sell them outside
Harmondsworth before 1066.

In SPELTHORNE Hundred

2   Hertald of Holy Trinity now holds 1 hide from the King. Land
for ½ plough.

1 villager who holds it.

Meadow for ½ plough.

Value of this land, 10s; when acquired the same; before 1066 the
same.

Golding, Earl Harold's man, held this land; he could not sell or
grant without his permission.

6   LAND OF BARKING CHURCH

In OSSULSTONE Hundred

1 M. The Abbess of Barking holds TYBURN* from the King. It answers
for 5 hides. Land for 3 ploughs. In lordship 2 hides; 1 plough
there. The villagers have 2 ploughs.

2 villagers with ½ hide; 1 villager with ½ virgate; 2 smallholders
with 10 acres; 3 cottagers.

Pasture for the village livestock; woodland, 50 pigs; from
grazing, 40d.

In total, value 52s; when acquired the same; before 1066, 100s.

This manor always lay and lies in (the lands of) Barking Church.

TERRA ROGERIJ COMITIS. *SPELETŌRNE HVND.*

.VII. **R**ogeri comes teñ in Hatone . I . hid 7 dim . Tra . I . car .
7 ibi . ē . Duo uilti teneN hanc trā . p̄tū . I . car . H̄ tra
ual . xv . fol . Q̄do recep̄ . fimil . T.R.E: xx . fol . Duo fochi
tenuer eā . hōes Albti Lotharienfis eraN . uende 7 dare potaN .
Modo appofita . ē in Colehā . ubi ñ erat . T.R.E.

ꝏ *HANEWORDE* ꝑ v . hid fe defd . Robt teñ de Rogerio com'
Tra . III . car . In dñio . I . car 7 dim . Vilti . II . car 7 dim . Ibi
. I . uilts de . I . hida . 7 v . uilti q̄fq̄ de . I . uirg . 7 II . uilti de . I . uirg .
7 II . cot . P̄tū . I . car . Pafta ad pecuñ uillæ . Int tot ual
xL . fol . Q̄do recep̄ . fimil . T.R.E: Lx . fol . Hoc ꝏ tenuit
Vlf hufcarl regis . E.   *HELETHORNE HVND.*

Comes Rog teñ in Hermodefuuorde . I . hid . Tra . I . car .
Ibi . ē dim car . 7 dim poteft fieri . Duo uilti teneN h trā .
Decē fol ualuit 7 ualet . Hanc tenuit Aluuin hō Wigot .
7 potuit facere qd uoluit . Modo jacet in Colehā . ubi
ñ jacuit . T . R . E .

ꝏ *HERDINTONE* ꝑ . x . hid fe defd .
Alured 7 Olaf teneN de comite Rḡ .
Tra . ē . vi . car . In dñio . II . car . m̄ . 7 uilti hñt . III . car .
7 IIII . poteft fieri . Ibi pbr dim h̄ . 7 xII . uilti q̄fq̄ unā
uirg . 7 IIII . uilti q̄fq̄ dim uirg . 7 II . bord de . xI . ac .
7 vIII . cot . 7 I . feru . P̄tū . II . car . In totis ualent ual
c . fol . Q̄do recep̄ . fimilit . T . R . E: vIII . lib . Hoc ꝏ . tenuit
Wigot . 7 de hac tra tenuit . I . fochi . II . hid . ñ pot uende
fine ej licentia .

ꝏ *COLEHAM* . ꝑ . vIII . hid fe defd . Rogeri com tenet .
Tra . vII . car . In dñio . vi . hidæ . 7 ibi funt . III . car . 7 uilti

SPELTHORNE Hundred

1   Earl Roger holds 1½ hides in HATTON. Land for 1 plough; it is there.
     2 villagers hold this land.
     Meadow for 1 plough.
     Value of this land 15s; when acquired the same; before 1066, 20s.
         2 Freemen held it; they were Albert of Lorraine's men; they
     could sell or grant. Now it is placed in Colham, where it was not
     before 1066.

2 M. HANWORTH   answers for 5 hides. Robert holds it from Earl Roger.
     Land for 3 ploughs. In lordship 1½ ploughs. The villagers, 2½ ploughs.
         1 villager with 1 hide; 5 villagers with 1 virgate each;
         2 villagers with 1 virgate; 2 cottagers.
     Meadow for 1 plough; pasture for the village livestock.
     In total, value 40s; when acquired the same; before 1066, 60s.
         Ulf, one of King Edward's Guards, held this manor.

ELTHORNE Hundred

3   In HARMONDSWORTH Earl Roger holds 1 hide. Land for 1 plough; ½
     plough there; ½ possible.
         2 villagers hold this land.
     The value was and is 10s.
         Alwin, Wigot's man, held it; he could do with it as he would. Now
     it lies in (the lands of) Colham, where it did not lie before 1066.

4 M. HARLINGTON answers for 10 hides. Alfred and Olaf hold it from
     Earl Roger. Land for 6 ploughs. Now in lordship 2 ploughs.
     The villagers have 3 ploughs; a fourth possible.
         A priest, ½ hide; 12 villagers, 1 virgate each; 4 villagers, ½
         virgate each; 2 smallholders with 11 acres; 8 cottagers; 1 slave.
     Meadow for 2 ploughs.
     Total value 100s; when acquired the same; before 1066 £8.
         Wigot held this manor. 1 Freeman held 2 hides of this land;
     he could not sell without his permission.

5 M. COLHAM* answers for 8 hides. Earl Roger holds it. Land for 7 ploughs.
     In lordship 6 hides; 3 ploughs there. The villagers have 3 ploughs.

hnt . iii . car . Ibi . vi . uilli . qfq̇ de . i . uirg̓ . 7 alij . or . de

ii . uirg . Pƀr . i . hid . 7 x . borđ qſq̇ de . v . ac . 7 iiii . cot .

7 viii . ſerui . Ibi . ii . molini de . xli . ſoł . 7 dim moliñ de

v . ſoł . p̊tū . iii . car . Paſta ad pecuñ uillæ . Silua . cccc .

porc̓ . 7 i . arpeñ uineæ . In totis ualent uał viii . liƀ . Q̇do

recep̄ . vi . liƀ . T . R . E . x . liƀ . Hoc m̃ tenuit Wigot de rege . E .

m̃ HILLENDONE . p̊ . iiii . hid | Rog com ten . Tra . ē . ii . car .

In dñio . ii . hidæ . 7 i . car pot fieri . Viłłi hñt . i . car̓ . Ibi . ii .

uiłłi de dim ħ . 7 ii . borđ . de . x . ac̓ . 7 i . cot . Duo francig̓ .

. i . hiđ 7 dim . ſub iſtis manent . iii . hões . P̊tū . iiii . boƀꝝ .

Silua mille porc̓ . De . i . guort . v . ſoł . In totis ualent

uał . iii . liƀ . Q̇do recep̄ . ſimilit̓ . T . R . E . iiii . liƀ . Hoc m̃

tenuit Vłf teign̓ . R . E . 7 potuit de eo facere qđ uoluit .

m̃ DALLEGA teñ Alnod de Rogerio comite . p̊ . iii . hiđ ſe defđ .

Tra . ē . ii . car̓ . In dñio . i . car̓ . 7 uiłłi hñt . i . car̓ . Ibi . iiii .

uiłłi qſq̇ de . i . urg̓ . 7 iiii . borđ de . v . ac̓ . P̊tū . vi . boū .

Paſta ad pecuñ uille . Silua . xv . porc̓ . Int totū uał

xxx . ſoł . Q̇do recep̄ . ſimilit̓ . T . R . E . lx . ſoł . Hoc m̃ jacet

in Coleħā ubi ñ fuit . T . R . E . Goduin alſit tenuit ħo Wigoti .

7 potuit de eo facere qđ uoluit .

129 b   m̃ TICHEHA p̊ . ix . hiđ 7 dim̃ ſe defđ . Tres milites 7 . i .

Anglic̓ teneꞃ de Rog com̓ . Tra . c̄ . vi . car̓ . Ibi ſuꞃ . iiii .

car̓ . 7 ii . adhuc poſſ . ee . Ibi . vi . uiłłi de . i . hiđ . 7 alij

. ii . de . i . ħ 7 i . uirg̓ . 7 alij . ii . de . ii . uirg̓ . 7 iiii . borđ

de . xx . ac̓ . 7 iii . cot . P̊tū . iiii . car̓ . Paſta ad pecuñ

uillæ . Silua . cc . porc̓ . In totis ualent uał . iiii . liƀ .

Q̇do recep̄ . ſimił . T . R . E . vi . liƀ . De ħ m̃ tenuit Tochi . ii . ħ .

huſcarle regis . E . fuit . 7 ii . ſochi . ii . ħ 7 i . uirg̓ . hões

Vluuardi fueꞃ . 7 Aluuin . i . ħ 7 iii . uirg̓ . hō Vłſi fit Manni fuit .

Vendere potueꞃ quo uolueꞃ . T . R . E . Ħ tra tota jacet

m̃ in Coleħā . ubi ñ fuit . T . R . E .

6 villagers, 1 virgate each; 4 others with 2 virgates; a priest,
  1 hide; 10 smallholders with 5 acres each; 4 cottagers; 8 slaves.
2 mills at 41s; ½ mill at 5s; meadow for 3 ploughs; pasture
  for the village livestock; woodland, 400 pigs; 1 *arpent* of vines.
Total value £8; when acquired £6; before 1066 £10.
Wigot held this manor from King Edward.

6 M. HILLINGDON answers for 4 hides. Earl Roger holds it. Land for 2
ploughs. In lordship 2 hides; 1 plough possible. The villagers have 1
plough.
  2 villagers with ½ hide; 2 smallholders with 10 acres; 1 cottager;
    2 Frenchmen with 1½ hides; 3 men dwell under them.
  Meadow for 4 oxen; woodland, 1000 pigs; from 1 weir, 5s.
Total value £3; when acquired the same; before 1066 £4.
  Ulf, a thane of King Edward's, held this manor and could do
with it as he would.

7 M. Alnoth holds DAWLEY from Earl Roger. It answers for 3 hides.
Land for 2 ploughs. In lordship 1 plough. The villagers have 1
plough.
  4 villagers with 1 virgate each; 4 smallholders with 5 acres.
  Meadow for 6 oxen; pasture for the village livestock; woodland,
    15 pigs.
In total, value 30s; when acquired the same; before 1066, 60s.
  This manor lies in (the lands of) Colham, where it was not before
1066. Godwin [son of?] Aelfeth,* Wigot's man, held it and could
do with it as he would.

8 M. ICKENHAM answers for 9½ hides. 3 men-at-arms and 1 Englishman 129 b
hold it from Earl Roger. Land for 6 ploughs; 4 ploughs there; a
further 2 possible.
  6 villagers with 1 hide; 2 others with 1 hide and 1 virgate; 2
    others with 2 virgates; 4 smallholders with 20 acres; 3 cottagers.
  Meadow for 4 ploughs; pasture for the village livestock; woodland,
    200 pigs.
Total value £4; when acquired the same; before 1066 £6.
  Toki held 2 hides of this manor; he was one of King Edward's Guards.
2 Freemen held 2 hides and 1 virgate; they were Wulfward's men.
Alwin held 1 hide and 3 virgates; he was Ulf son of Manni's man;
they could sell where they would before 1066. Now the whole of
this land lies in (the lands of) Colham, where it was not before 1066.

Comes de moriton̕ tenet in Leleha̅.ɪɪ.hidas.

7 abb de fifca̅no de eọ.Tra̕.ɪ.car̕ 7 dim̕.7 ibi fuꝡ̕
Sex uilli de dim̕ ħ.7 vɪɪ.cot̕.Ptu̅.ɪ.car̕ 7 dim̕.
Pafta̕ ad pecun̕ uillæ.Ħ tra̕ ual.xʟ.fot.Qdo recep̄
7 T.R.E.⸵ʟ.fot.Hanc tra̅ tenuit p̄fect̕ de Stanes
fub abbe de Weftmonaft.n̅ potuit dare 𝑡 uende̕
ext̕ Stanes p̄ter abbis licentia̅.

In Exeforde ten̕ ifde̅ comes.ɪ.hid̕.Tra̕.e̅.ɪ.car̕.
7 ibi.e̅.Ptu̅.ɪ.car̕.Ħ tra̕ ual xɪɪɪɪ.fot.Qdo recep̄.
fimit.T.R.E.⸵xx.fot.Hanc tenuit Aluric hō abbis
de Certefi.7 potuit inde facere qđ uoluit.Modo
appofita.e̅ in Chenetone Ꝏ̅ comitis.ubi n̅ fuit.T.R.E.
Soca ů jacebat in Stanes.

In Bedefunt ten̕ ifde̅ com̕.ɪɪ.hid̕.Tra̕.e̅.ɪ.car̕.Ibi
m̊ dim̕ car̕.7 dim̕ poteft fieri.Ibi.ɪ.uilłs.vɪɪɪ.ac̕.
7 q̊da̅ miles dim̕ hid̕.Ptu̅.ɪ.bou̕.Pafta̕ ad pecun̕.
Ħ tra̕ ual.v.fot.Qdo recep̄.fimit.T.R.E.⸵xx.fot.
Hanc tra̕ tenuit Gouti Hufcarle Heraldi.7 potuit
inde face̕ qđ uoluit.Ħ tra̕ jacuit 7 jacet in Feltehā.

Ꝏ̅ *FELTEHA̅* ten̕ ifd̕ comes ꝑ xɪɪ.hid̕ fe defd̕.Tra̕.e̅
x.car̕.In dnio.vɪ.hide̕.7 ibi.e̅.ɪ.car̕.7 ɪɪɪ.adhuc
pofs.ee̕.Vilłi h̅nt.vɪɪɪ.car̕.Ibi.xɪɪɪɪ.uilłi qfq̊
de.ɪ.uirga.7 alij.v.qfq̊ de dim̕ uirg̕.7 ɪɪ.ferui.
Ptu̅.x.car̕.Pafta ad pecun̕ uillæ.Int totu̅ ual
vɪ.lib.Qdo recep̄.ɪɪɪɪ.lib.T.R.E.vɪɪɪ.lib.Hoc Ꝏ̅
tenueꝶ.ɪɪ.teigni.Vn̊ hoꝛ hō.R.E.q̊.v.hiđ habuit.ꝑ.ɪ.Ꝏ̅
7 alt̕ hō Heraldi.vɪɪ.hiđ ꝑ.ɪ.Ꝏ̅.7 potueꝶ inde
facere qđ uolueꝶ.

LAND OF THE COUNT OF MORTAIN

In SPELTHORNE Hundred

1   The Count of Mortain holds 2 hides in LALEHAM, and the Abbot of
Fecamp from him. Land for 1½ ploughs; they are there.
> 6 villagers with ½ hide; 7 cottagers.
> Meadow for 1½ ploughs; pasture for the village livestock.

Value of this land, 40s; when acquired and before 1066, 50s.
The Reeve of Staines held this land under the Abbot of Westminster;
he could not grant or sell it outside Staines except with the
Abbot's permission.

The Count also holds*

2   in ASHFORD, 1 hide. Land for 1 plough; it is there.
> Meadow for 1 plough.

Value of this land, 14s; when acquired the same; before 1066, 20s.
Aelfric, the Abbot of Chertsey's man, held it, and could do what
he would with it. Now it is placed in the Count's manor of Kempton,
where it was not before 1066; but the jurisdiction lay in Staines.

3   in (EAST) BEDFONT, 2 hides. Land for 1 plough; ½ plough there
now; ½ possible.
> 1 villager, 8 acres; a man-at-arms, ½ hide.
> Meadow for 1 ox; pasture for the livestock.

Value of this land, 5s; when acquired the same; before 1066, 20s.
Gauti, one of Earl Harold's Guards, held this land, and could do
what he would with it. This land lay and lies in (the lands of) Feltham.

4 M. FELTHAM. It answers for 12 hides. Land for 10 ploughs. In lordship 6
hides; 1 plough there; a further 3 possible. The villagers have 8 ploughs.*
> 14 villagers with 1 virgate each; 5 others with ½ virgate each; 2
> slaves.
> Meadow for 10 ploughs; pasture for the village livestock.

In total, value £6; when acquired £4; before 1066 £8.
Two thanes held this manor; one of them, King Edward's man,
had 5 hides as 1 manor; the other, Earl Harold's man, had 7 hides
as 1 manor; they could do what they would with them.

Ⓜ *Chenetone* teñ iſd com.p.v.hiđ ſe defđ.Tra
eſt.v.car.In dñio.11.hiđ 7 dim uirg.7 ibi.e̅.1.car.
7 alia pot fieri.Viłłi hn̄t.111.car.Ibi.vi.uiłłi qſq̢
de.1.uirg.7 alij.viii.qſq̢ de dim uirg.7 111.bord.
de.1.uirg.7 11.ſerui.p̃tu.v.car.Paſta ad pec uillæ.
7 viii.arpenñ uineæ nouit plantatæ.Int tot ual
1111.lib̄.Q̣do recep̃.111.lib̄.T.R.E.́vi.lib̄.Hoc Ⓜ tenuit
Wluuard teign̄.R.E.7 potuit facere qđ uoluit.

In Gare iivnd.

129 c Ⓜ *Stanmere* teñ iſd com p 1x.hiđ 7 dim ſe defđ.
Tra.e̅.vii.car.In dñio.vi.hiđ 7 dim.7 11.car fuɲ ibi.
7 alia pot fieri.Viłłi hn̄t.1.car 7 dim.7 11.car 7 dim
poıs fieri.Ibi p̄br h̄t dim hid.7 1111.uiłłi qſq̢ de.1.uirg.
7 alij.11.de.1.uirg.7 111.cot de.x..ac.7 alij.111.de.1.ac̃.
Paſta ad pec uillæ.Silua octing porc.7 de Herbagia
xii.den.In totis ualent ual.lx.ſoł.Q̣do recep̃.x.ſoł.
T.R.E.́x.lib̄.Hoc Ⓜ tenuit Edmer teign̄.R.E.

.IX. Terra Goisfr̄ De Mänevile Osvlvestane hd̄.
Ⓜ Goisfriđ de Manneuilla.teñ *Eia*.p x.hiđ ſe
defđ.Tra.e̅.viii.car.In dñio.v.hiđ.7 ibi ſunt.11.car.
Viłłi hn̄t.v.car.7 vi.poteſt fieri.Ibi.1.uiłłs dim h̄.
7 1111.uiłłi.qſq̢ de.1.uirg.7 alij x1111.qſq̢ de dim uirg.
7 1111.borđ de.1.uirg.7 1.cot.P̃tu.viii.car.7 de feno.
lx.ſoł.De paſta.vii.ſoł.In totis ualent ual.viii.lib̄.
Q̣do recep̃.vi.lib̄.T.R.E.́xii.lib̄.Hoc Ⓜ tenuit
Herald fili̇ Radulfi comitis.quē cuſtodieb̄ regina
Eddid cū Ⓜ ea die q̃ rex Edw fuit uiuus 7 mortuus.
Poſtea Wiłłs camerari̇ tenuit de regina in feudo .p.111.́

129 b, c

5 M. **KEMPTON.** It answers for 5 hides. Land for 5 ploughs. In lordship 2 hides and ½ virgate; 1 plough there; another possible. The villagers have 3 ploughs.

 6 villagers with 1 virgate each; 8 others with ½ virgate each;
  3 smallholders with 1 virgate; 2 slaves.
 Meadow for 5 ploughs; pasture for the village livestock;
  8 *arpents* of newly planted vines.
In total, value £4; when acquired £3; before 1066 £6.

 Wulfward Wight, a thane of King Edward's, held this manor, and could do what he would with it.

In GORE Hundred

6 M. **STANMORE.** It answers for 9½ hides. Land for 7 ploughs. In   129 c
lordship 6½ hides; 2 ploughs there; another possible. The villagers have 1½ ploughs; 2½ ploughs possible.

 A priest has ½ hide; 4 villagers with 1 virgate each;
  2 others with 1 virgate; 3 cottagers with 10 acres; 3 others
  with 1 acre.
 Pasture for the village livestock; woodland, 800 pigs; from
  grazing, 12d.
Total value 60s; when acquired 10s; before 1066 £10.

 Edmer Ator*, a thane of King Edward's, held this manor.

9   LAND OF GEOFFREY DE MANDEVILLE

OSSULSTONE Hundred

1 M. Geoffrey de Mandeville holds EBURY.* It answers for 10 hides. Land for 8 ploughs. In lordship 5 hides; 2 ploughs there. The villagers have 5 ploughs; a sixth possible.

 1 villager, ½ hide; 4 villagers with 1 virgate each; 14 others
  with ½ virgate each; 4 smallholders with 1 virgate; 1 cottager.
 Meadow for 8 ploughs; from hay 60s; from pasture 7s.
Total value £8; when acquired £6; before 1066 £12.

 Harold son of Earl Ralph held this manor. Queen Edith had charge of him, with the manor, in 1066; afterwards, William the Chamberlain

lib p annū de firma.7 poſt mortē reginæ eod m̄ tenuit
de rege. Nc̄ ſunt. IIII. anni qđ Wilłs c̄m̄ amiſit.7 inde
n̄ eſt reddita firma regis. id eſt. XII. lib.

In eod Hund ten Radulf⁹ de Goisfr̄. I. hid 7 dimid.
T̛ra. I. car̛.7 ibi eſt.7 IIII. bord. de. XIIII. ac̛.7 I. ſerú.
P̛tū. I. car̄. Paſta ad pecuñ.7 XIII. den̛. Nem ad ſepes.
H̄ t̛ra uał. xx. ſoł. Q̇do recep̄.7 T.R.E.⸝ xxx. ſoł. Hanc t̛ra
tenuer̄. II. ſocħi regis. E. uende potuer̄ cui uoluer̄.

In ISENDONE ten Gulbt̛ de Goisf̛. dim hid. T̛ra. ē dim
car̛.7 ibi eſt.7 I. uiłłs 7 I. bord. H̄ t̛ra uał XII. ſoł. Q̇do
recep̄. ſimilit̛. T.R.E.⸝ xx. ſoł. Hanc tenuit Grim hō. R.E.
7 uende potuit.   IN HELETHORNE HD̄.

In GRENEFORDE ten̛ Ernulf⁹ de Goisf̛. III. hid. T̛ra. I. car̛
7 dim̛. Ibi. ē. I. car̛.7 dim car̛ poteſt fieri. Ibi. II. uiłłi de
dim̛ hida.7 II. cot̛.7 I. ſerú. Silua. XL. porc̛. H̄ t̛ra uał
xx. ſoł. Q̇do recep̄⸝ x. ſoł. T.R.E.⸝ xl. ſoł ⸝ Hanc t̛ra tenuer̄
II. ſocħi. Vn̛ hoꝛ canonic̛ fuit S̄ Pauli. II. hid habuit.
potuit inde facere qđ uoluit. Alt̛ hō fuit Anſgari ſtalri.
n̄ potuit dare p̄ter ej⁹ licentiā.

In ead uilla ten Anſgot̛ de Goisfr̄ dim̛ hid. T̛ra. II. boú.
H̄ t̛ra uał. III. ſoł.7 qdo recep̄ 7 T.R.E.⸝ ſimilit̛. Hanc
t̛rā tenuit Azor. hō Anſgari ſtalri fuit. n̄ potuit
uende ſine ej⁹ licentia.

In TICHEHĀ teneꝗ. II. Angli de Goisf̛. III. hid 7 dim̛. T̛ra
ē. II. car̛.7 ibi ſuꝗ. Tres uiłłi q̇ſꝗ de dim̛ uirg̛.7 v. bord.
p̄tū. II. car̄. Paſta ad pec̛ uillæ. Silua. XL. porc̛. H̄ t̛ra
uał. xxx. ſoł. Q̇do recep̄⸝ ſimił. T.R.E.⸝ lx. ſoł. H̄anc t̛rā
tenuer̄. II. ſocħi. un̛ hoꝛ hō Aſgari ſtalri fuit.7 I. hid

held it from the Queen, as a Holding, for £3 a year in revenue;
after the Queen's death he held it in the same way from the King.
William lost the manor 4 years ago; since then the King's revenue,
i.e. £12, has not been paid.

2   In the same Hundred Ralph holds 1½ hides from Geoffrey.
Land for 1 plough; it is there.
    4 smallholders with 14 acres; 1 slave.
    Meadow for 1 plough; pasture for the livestock, and 13d too;
      wood for fences.
Value of this land, 20s; when acquired and before 1066, 30s.
    2 Freemen of King Edward's held this land; they could sell to
whom they would.

3   In ISLINGTON Wulfbert* holds ½ hide from Geoffrey.
Land for ½ plough; it is there.
    1 villager; 1 smallholder.
Value of this land, 12s; when acquired the same; before 1066, 20s.
    Grim, King Edward's man held it and could sell.

In ELTHORNE Hundred

4   In GREENFORD Arnulf holds 3 hides from Geoffrey. Land for 1½
ploughs; 1 plough there; ½ plough possible.
    2 villagers with ½ hide; 2 cottagers; 1 slave.
    Woodland, 40 pigs.
Value of this land, 20s; when acquired 10s; before 1066, 40s.
    2 Freemen held this land; one of them was a Canon of St. Paul's; he
had 2 hides and could do what he would with them; the other was
Asgar the Constable's man; he could not grant except with his
permission.

5   In the same village Ansgot holds ½ hide from Geoffrey.
Land for 2 oxen
    Value of this land, 3s; when acquired and before 1066 the same.
    Azor held this land. He was Asgar the Constable's man;
he could not sell without his permission.

6   In ICKENHAM 2 Englishmen hold 3½ hides from Geoffrey. Land for 2
ploughs; they are there.
    3 villagers with ½ virgate each; 5 smallholders.
    Meadow for 2 ploughs; pasture for the village livestock;
      woodland, 40 pigs.
Value of this land, 30s; when acquired the same; before 1066, 60s.
    2 Freemen held* this land; one of them was Asgar the

habuit.ñ potuit uende p̄t ej licent.7 alt hō Leuuini fuit.

.ii hid 7 dim habuit.7 potuit uende.T.R.E.

Ⓜ *Northala* teñ Goisf de manneuilla. p̄ xv.hid se
defd.Tra.ē.x.car.In dñio.viii.hid 7 ibi sunt.ii.car.
Viłłi hñt.vi.car.7 ii.car poſſ fieri.Ibi p̄br dim hid
7 i.uiłł.i.ħ.7 alij.v.q̄ſq̄ dim ħ.7 alij.viii.q̄ſq̄.i.uirg
7 alij.viii.q̄ſq̄ dim uirg.7 iii.cot 7 vi.serui.Paſta ad
pecuñ.Silua.cc.porc.In totis ualent uał.x.liƀ.Q̄do
receꝑ.v.liƀ.T.R.E.xii.liƀ.Hoc Ⓜ tenuit Asgar ſtałr.

Delmetone Hvnd.

Ⓜ *Adelmetone* teñ Goisf de mañ. p̄ xxxv.hid se def.
Tra.ē.xxvi.car.In dñio.xvi.hidæ.7 iiii.car.Viłłi
hñt.xxii.car.Ibi uñ uiłłs de.i.ħ.7 alij.iii.q̄ſq̄ dim
hid.7 xx.uiłłi q̄ſq̄ de.i.uirg.7 alij xxiiii.q̄ſq̄ dim
uirg.7 ix.borđ.de.iii.uirg.7 iiii.borđ q̄ſq̄ de.v.ac
7 iiii.borđ q̄ſq̄ iiii.ac.7 iiii.cot de.iiii.ac.x.cot.
7 iiii.uiłł de.i.hid 7 i.uirg.7 iiii.serui.Ibi.i.moliñ
x.solid.P̄tū.xxvi.car.7 xxv.sol de suꝑ plus.Paſta
ad pec.   Silua.ii.mił porc.7 xii.sol de redditis
siluæ   7 pasturæ.In totis ualent uał.xl.liƀ.
Q̄do receꝑ.xx.liƀ.T.R.E.xl.liƀ.Hoc Ⓜ tenuit
Asgar ſtałr.R.E. Ad hoc Ⓜ jacuit 7 jacet una Berew
quæ uocat Mimes.7 ē apꝑciata cū Manerio.

Ⓜ *Enefelde* teñ Goisf de Maneuilla p̄ xxx.hid se defd.
Tra.xxiiii.car.In dñio.xiiii.hide.7 ibi suŋ.iiii.car.
Viłłi hñt.xvi.car.Ibi uñ uiłłs de.i.hid.7 iii.uiłłi
q̄ſq̄ de dim ħ.Prƀr.i.uirg.7 xvii.uiłłi q̄ſq̄.i.uirg.
7 xxxvi.uiłłi q̄ſq̄ dim uirg.7 xx.borđ de.i.hid 7 i.uirg.
7 vii.cot de xxiii.ac.7 v.cot de.vii.ac.7 xviii.cot.

Constable's man; he had 1 hide and could not sell except
with his permission; the other was Earl Leofwin's
man; he had 2½ hides and could sell before 1066.

7 M. Geoffrey de Mandeville holds NORTHOLT. It answers for 15 hides.
Land for 10 ploughs. In lordship 8 hides; 2 ploughs there.
The villagers have 6 ploughs; 2 ploughs possible.
   A priest, ½ hide; 1 villager, 1 hide; 5 others, ½ hide each;
      8 others, 1 virgate each; 8 others, ½ virgate each; 3 cottagers;
      6 slaves.
   Pasture for the livestock; woodland, 200 pigs.
Total value £10; when acquired £5; before 1066 £12.
Asgar the Constable held this manor.

EDMONTON Hundred
8 M. Geoffrey de Mandeville holds EDMONTON. It answers for 35 hides.
Land for 26 ploughs. In lordship 16 hides; 4 ploughs. The
villagers have 22 ploughs.
   1 villager with 1 hide; 3 others, ½ hide each; 20 villagers
      with 1 virgate each; 24 others, ½ virgate each; 9 smallholders
      with 3 virgates; 4 smallholders with 5 acres each; 4 smallholders
      with 4 acres each; 4 cottagers with 4 acres; 10 cottagers; 4
      villagers with 1 hide and 1 virgate; 4 slaves.
   1 mill, 10s; meadow for 26 ploughs, and 25s over and above;
      pasture for the livestock; woodland, 2000 pigs; from the
      payments of the woodland and pasture, 12s.
Total value £40; when acquired £20; before 1066 £40.
   Asgar, King Edward's Constable, held this manor. An outlier
called (SOUTH) MIMMS lay and lies in (the lands of) this manor;
it is assessed with the manor.

9 M. Geoffrey de Mandeville holds ENFIELD. It answers for 30 hides.
Land for 24 ploughs. In lordship 14 hides. 4 ploughs there.
The villagers have 16 ploughs.
   1 villager with 1 hide; 3 villagers with ½ hide each; a
      priest, 1 virgate; 17 villagers, 1 virgate each; 36 villagers,
      ½ virgate each; 20 smallholders with 1 hide and 1 virgate; 7
      cottagers with 23 acres; 5 cottagers with 7 acres;

7 vi . ſerui . Ibi . i . moliñ . x . ſolid . De Piſcinis . viii . ſot . P̃tu
xxiiii . caŕ . 7 xxv . ſot de ſuꝑ plus . Paſta ad peċ uillæ.
Silua . ii . mit porċ . De ſilua 7 paſta . xliii . ſot . 7 parċ
eſt ibi . In totis ualent uat . l . lib̃ . Q̇do receꝑ.' xx . lib̃.
T.R.E.' l . lib̃ . Hoc ⱮƆ tenuit Aſgar ſtalŕ regis Edw.
In hac tra fueŕ . v . ſochi de . vi . hid . quas potueŕ
dare ⱡ uende ſine licentia dño₇ ſuo₇.

.X. TERRA ERNVLFI DE HESDING *HELETORNE HVND.*

ⱮƆ Ernvlf de heſding tenet *Rislepe* . ꝑ xxx . hiđ
ſe defđ . Tra . e̅ xx . caŕ . In dñio xi . hidæ . 7 ibi ſuꞃ . iii .
caŕ . Int franċ 7 uitt . ſuꞃ . xii . caŕ . 7 v . adhuc poſſ̃ fieri.
Ibi pb̃r dim̃ hiđ . 7 ii . uitti de . i . hiđ . 7 xvii . uitti q̇ſq̇₇
. i . uirg̃ . 7 x . uitti q̇ſq̇₇ dim̃ uirg̃ . 7 vii . borđ q̇ſq̇₇ . iiii .
aċ . 7 viii . cot . 7 iiii . ſerui . 7 iiii . francig de . iii . hid .
7 i . uirg̃ . Paſta ad peċ uillæ . Parċ eſt ibi feraru̅ Silua
ticaru̅ . Silua mille 7 q̇ngent̃ porċ . 7 xx . den . In totis
ualent uat . xx . lib̃ . Q̇do receꝑ.' xii . lib̃ . T.R.E.' xxx . lib̃
Hoc ⱮƆ tenuit Wluuard̃ teigñ . R . E . potuit uende
cui uoluit

ⱮƆ In Chingeſberie teñ Albold̃ de Ernulfo . vii . hiđ
7 dim̃.

Tra . e̅ . vii . caŕ . In dñio . ii . caŕ . 7 uitti . v . caŕ . Ibi . viii . uitti
q̇ſq̇₇ de . i . uirg̃ . 7 iii . uitti . q̇ſq̇₇ dim̃ uirg̃ . Pb̃r . i . uirg̃ . 7 v . borđ
quiſq̇₇ de . v . aċ . Ibi . i . moliñ . iii . ſolid̃ . P̃tu dim̃ caŕ . Silua
mille porċ . 7 xx . ſot . In totis ualent uat . iiii . lib̃ . Q̇do receꝑ.'
xx . ſot . T.R.E.' vi . lib̃ . Hoc ⱮƆ tenuit Wluuard̃ teigñ . R . E.

18 cottagers; 6 slaves.

1 mill, 10s; from the fishponds, 8s; meadow for 24 ploughs, and 25s over and above; pasture for the village livestock; woodland, 2000 pigs; from woodland and pasture, 43s; a park.

Total value £50; when acquired £20; before 1066 £50.

Asgar, King Edward's Constable, held this manor. On this land were 5 Freemen with 6 hides which they could grant or sell without their lords'* permission.

10   LAND OF ARNULF OF HESDIN

ELTHORNE Hundred

1 M. Arnulf of Hesdin holds RUISLIP. It answers for 30 hides. Land for 20 ploughs. In lordship 11 hides; 3 ploughs there. There are 12 ploughs between the Frenchmen and the villagers; a further 5 possible.

A priest, ½ hide; 2 villagers with 1 hide; 17 villagers, 1 virgate each; 10 villagers, ½ virgate each; 7 smallholders, 4 acres each; 8 cottagers; 4 slaves; 4 Frenchmen with 3 hides and 1 virgate.

Pasture for the village livestock; a park for woodland beasts; woodland, 1500 pigs, and 20d too.

Total value £20; when acquired £12; before 1066 £30.

Wulfward Wight, a thane of King Edward's, held this manor; he could sell to whom he would.

[GORE Hundred]

2 M. In KINGSBURY Albold holds 7½ hides from Arnulf.

Land for 7 ploughs. In lordship 2 ploughs. The villagers, 5 ploughs.

8 villagers with 1 virgate each; 3 villagers, ½ virgate each;   130 a
a priest, 1 virgate; 5 smallholders with 5 acres each.

1 mill, 3s; meadow for ½ plough; woodland, 1000 pigs, and 20s too.

Total value £4; when acquired 20s; before 1066 £6.

Wulfward Wight, a thane of King Edward's, held this manor.

Walterivs fili⁹ Other tenet de rege *Stanwelle.*

p̄ xv.hið ſe defð.Tra.e̅.x.car̄.In dn̅io.iii.hidæ.7 iii.car̄.

Int franc̄ 7 uiłł.x.car̄.Ibi.i.uiłł de.i.hid.7 viii.uiłłi.qſq̄

dim̄ hið.7 x.uiłłi qſq̄.i.uirg.7 viii.uiłł qſq̄ dim̄ uirg.7 iiii.

borð de xxviii.ac.7 ii.cot 7 viii.ſerui.7 ii.milit.ii.hid 7 dim̄.

7 ſub eis.vi.borð mane͡ſ.Ibi.iiii.mol de lxx.ſol.7 cccc.

Anguiłł.xxv.min.De.iii.gorz.mille Anguiłł.p̄tū.xii.car̄.

Paſta ad pec uillæ.Silua.c.porc̄.In totis ualent uał

xiiii.liɓ.Q̣do recep̄.vi.liɓ.T.R.E.xiiii.liɓ.Hoc ꝏ

tenuit Azor Huſcarle.R.E.7 potuit inde face qð uoluit.

In Bedefunde ten̄ Ricard de Walterio.f.Otheri.x.hið

p̄.i.manerio.Tra.e̅.v.car̄.In dn̅io.i.car̄.7 iiii.car̄ int

franc̄ 7 uiłł.Ibi.iiii.uiłłi de.i.hida.7 alij.iiii.qſq̄ dim̄ uirg.

7 iii.borð de.xiii.ac.qdā miles.ii.hid.P̄tū.ii.bob.

Paſta ad pec uillæ.Int totū uał.iiii.liɓ.Q̣do recep̄.

xx.ſol.T.R.E.vi.liɓ.De hoc ꝏ ten̄ Azor.viii.hid

7 dim̄.7 fuit Berew in Stanuuelle.7 iii.ſoch habuer̄.i.hid

7 dim̄.Vn̄⁹ ho᷄ hō.R.E.fuit.Alt̄ hō Leuuini.Tci⁹ hō Azoris.

qſq̄ habuit dim̄ hid.7 potuer̄ uende l̄ dare.7 ad ꝏ n̄ p̄ti

nuer̄.T.R.E.

In Weſt bedefund ten̄ Walter⁹ de mucedent de Waltero ⸱f.Other

viii.hið p̄ uno ꝏ.Tra.e̅.iiii.car̄.In dn̅io.i.car̄.7 uiłłi

hn̅t.iii.car̄.Ibi.ii.uiłłi de.iiii.hid.7 ii.uiłłi de.ii.uirg.

7 ii.uiłłi de.i.uirg.7 i.borð de.v.ac.Pɓr.i.uirg.7 i.cot

de.v.ac.7 ii.ſerui.P̄tū.ii.boū.Paſta ad pec uillæ.Int

totū uał.iii.liɓ.Q̣do recep̄.ſimilit̄.T.R.E.vi.liɓ.De hoc

ꝏ tenuit Brithmar.iiii.ħ.hō comitis Heraldi fuit.potuit

uende cui uoluit.7 ii.ſoch̄i tenuer̄.iiii.hid.hões Azoris

fuer̄.n̄ potuer̄ uende l̄ dare abſq̄ ej⁹ licentia.

11   LAND OF WALTER SON OF OTHERE

SPELTHORNE Hundred

1   Walter son of Othere holds STANWELL from the King. It answers for 15 hides. Land for 10 ploughs. In lordship 3 hides and 3 ploughs. 10 ploughs between the Frenchmen and the villagers.
    1 villager with 1 hide; 8 villagers, ½ hide each; 10 villagers, 1 virgate each; 8 villagers, ½ virgate each; 4 smallholders with 28 acres; 2 cottagers; 8 slaves; 2 men-at-arms, 2½ hides, and under them dwell 6 smallholders.
    4 mills at 70s, and 400 eels, less 25; 1000 eels from 3 weirs; meadow for 12 ploughs; pasture for the village livestock; woodland, 100 pigs.
Total value £14; when acquired £6; before 1066 £14.
    Azor, one of King Edward's Guards, held this manor, and could do what he would with it.

2   In (EAST) BEDFONT Richard holds 10 hides as 1 manor from Walter son of Othere. Land for 5 ploughs. In lordship 1 plough.
4 ploughs between the Frenchmen and the villagers.
    4 villagers with 1 hide; 4 others, ½ virgate each; 3 smallholders with 13 acres; a man-at-arms, 2 hides.
    Meadow for 2 oxen; pasture for the village livestock.
In total, value £4; when acquired 20s; before 1066 £6.
    Azor held 8½ hides of this manor; it was an outlier in Stanwell.
    3 Freemen had 1½ hides; one of them was King Edward's man, another Leofwin's, the third Azor's; each had ½ hide and could sell or grant. They did not belong to the manor before 1066.

3   In WEST BEDFONT Walter of *Mucedent* holds 8 hides as 1 manor from Walter son of Othere. Land for 4 ploughs. In lordship 1 plough.
The villagers have 3 ploughs.
    2 villagers with 4 hides; 2 villagers with 2 virgates; 2 villagers with 1 virgate; 1 smallholder with 5 acres; a priest with 1 virgate; 1 cottager with 5 acres; 2 slaves.
    Meadow for 2 oxen; pasture for the village livestock.
In total, value £3; when acquired, the same; before 1066 £6.
    Brictmer, Earl Harold's man, held 4 hides of this manor; he could sell to whom he would. 2 Freemen held 4 hides, they were Azor's men; they could not sell or grant without his permission.

In Haitone tēn Walter⁹ de mucedent de Waltero

unā hid 7 ꝛꝛꝛ.uirg.7 ꝛꝛꝛ.parte̅ de.ꝛ.uirg.Tra.e̅.ꝛ.car.

Ibi.e̅ dim car.7 dim car poteſt fieri.Ibi.ꝛ.uiłłs de.ꝛ.uirg.

7 ꝛꝛ.uirg de.ꝛ.uirg.7 ꝛ.borđ de.v.ac.Ptū.ꝛ.car.paſta

ad pecun.H̅ tra uał.xx.ſoł.Q̨do recep̃.ſimilit̃.T.R.E.

xxx.ſoł.Hanc tra̅ tenuer̃.ꝛꝛ.ſocħi.hōes Azoris fuer̃.non

potuer̃ uende p̃t ej licentiā.

.XII.TERRA WALTERIJ DE S̄ WALERI. *HONESLAVV.HVND.*

W̅ALTERIVS de S̄ Walarico tēn *GISTELESWORDE.*

ꝑ LXX.hiđ ſe defđ ſe̅p.Tra.e̅.LV.car.In dn̄io.vꝛ.

hiđ 7 dim.7 ibi ſunt.vꝛ.car.Int franc 7 uiłł.xxvꝛꝛꝛ.

car̃.7 adhuc.xꝛ.poſs fieri.Ibi pꝫr h̅t.ꝛꝛꝛ.uirg.7 Lꝛ.

uiłłi q̃ſq̨ de.ꝛ.uirg.7 xxꝛꝛꝛꝛ.uiłłi.q̃ſq̨ de dim uirg.

7 xvꝛꝛꝛ.uiłłi q̃ſq̨ dim uirg.7 vꝛ.cot.Franciɡ 7 q̨dā an

glicus.ꝛꝛꝛꝛ.hiđ.7 ſuꝛ̃ milites ꝑbati.Sub eis maneꝛ̃ int

130 b   uiłł 7 borđ.xꝛꝛ.7 vꝛ.uiłłi dn̄i q̨ teneꝛ̃.ꝛꝛ.hiđ 7 dim uirg.

Ibi.ꝛꝛ.molini de.x.ſoł.Ptū.xx.car.Paſta ad pecun

uillæ.Vnū gort 7 dim de xꝛꝛ.ſoł 7 vꝛꝛꝛ.den.Silua

q̃ngent porc.De herbagia.xꝛꝛ.den.In totis ualent

uał.Lxxꝛꝛ.lib.Q̨do recep̃.ſimilit̃.T.R.E.q̃t xx.lib

Hoc M̅ tenuit Algar.

M̅ *H̅AMNTONE* tēn iſđ Walteri⁹.ꝑ xxxv.hid ſe defđ.

Tra.e̅ xxv.car.In dn̄io.xvꝛꝛꝛ.hidæ.7 ꝛꝛꝛ.car.Viłłi

h̅nt.xvꝛꝛ.car.7 v.car adhuc poſs fieri.Ibi.xxx.uiłłi

q̃ſq̨ de.ꝛ.uirg.7 xꝛ.uiłłi de.ꝛꝛ.hid 7 dim.7 ꝛꝛꝛꝛ.borđ

q̃ſq̨ de dim uirg.Ptū.ꝛꝛꝛ.car.7 x.ſoł.Paſta ad pec

uillæ.De ſagenis 7 tractis in aq̨ temiſiæ.ꝛꝛꝛ.ſoł.In totis

ualent uał.xxxꝛx.lib.Q̨do recep̃.xx.lib.T.R.E.

xL.lib.Hoc M̅ tenuit Algarus.

4   In HATTON Walter of *Mucedent* holds 1 hide, 3 virgates, and the third
     part of 1 virgate from Walter son of Othere. Land for 1 plough;
     ½ plough there; ½ plough possible.
         1 villager with 1 virgate; 2 villagers* with 1 virgate;
         1 smallholder with 5 acres.
     Meadow for 1 plough; pasture for the livestock.
     Value of this land, 20s; when acquired the same; before 1066, 30s.
         2 Freemen held this land; they were Azor's men; they could not
     sell except with his permission.

12   LAND OF WALTER OF ST. VALERY

HOUNSLOW Hundred
1   Walter of St. Valery holds ISLEWORTH. It always answered for 70
     hides. Land for 55 ploughs. In lordship 6½ hides; 6 ploughs there.
     28 ploughs between the Frenchmen and the villagers; a further 11*
     possible.
         A priest has 3 virgates; 51 villagers with 1 virgate each;
         24 villagers with ½ virgate each; 18 villagers, ½ virgate each;
         6 cottagers. A Frenchman and an Englishman, 4 hides; they are
         proven* men-at-arms; under them dwell 12 of the villagers   130 b
         and smallholders, and 6 of the lord's villagers, who hold 2 hides
         and ½ virgate.
         2 mills at 10s; meadow for 20 ploughs; pasture for the village
         livestock; 1½ weirs at 12s 8d; woodland, 500 pigs; from
         grazing, 12d.
     Total value £72; when acquired the same; before 1066 £80.
     Earl Algar held this manor.

2 M. Walter also holds HAMPTON*. It answers for 35 hides. Land for 25
     ploughs. In lordship 18 hides and 3 ploughs. The villagers have
     17 ploughs; a further 5 ploughs possible.
         30 villagers with 1 virgate each; 11 villagers with 2½ hides;
         4 smallholders with ½ virgate each.
         Meadow for 3 ploughs, and 10s too; pasture for the village
             livestock; from fishing-nets and drag-nets in the river Thames, 3s.
     Total value £39; when acquired £20; before 1066 £40.
     Earl Algar held this manor.

Ⓜ RICARD⁹ filius Gisłebti comitis teñ *HEREFELLE.*

.p. v. hid se defd. Tra. e͂. v. car. In dñio. ii. hidæ.

7 ibi funt. ii. car. Vitti hñt. iii. car. Ibi pbr. hr̄

.i. uirg. 7 v. uitti q̇fq̧ de. i. uirg. 7 alij. v. q̇fq̧ dim

uirg. 7 vii. bord. q̇fq de. v. ac. 7 i. bord de. iii. ac.

7 iii. cot. 7 iii. ferui. Ibi. ii. molini de. xv. fot. De. iiii.

pifcinis. mille anguit. p̃tu. i. car. Pafta ad pecuñ

uitle. Sillua ad mille cc. porc. In totis ualent ual

xii. lib. Q̨do recep. viii. lib. T.R.E. xiiii. lib. Hoc Ⓜ

tenuit Goda comitiffa. T.R.E.

Ⓜ ROTBERT⁹ Gernon teñ de rege. ii. hid in *HERGO*

TESTANE. Tra. e͂. ii. car. 7 ibi funt. iii. car. Ibi. iiii.

uitti 7 vii. bord qui teneⁿ hanc tr̄a. 7 ual. xlv. fot.

Q̨do recep. xl. fot. T.R.E. l. fot. Hoc Ⓜ tenuit

Aluuin⁹ ho͂ regis E. uende potuit cui uoluit.

In Helethorne hund teñ Nigell⁹ de Rotbto Gernon

ii. hid. Tra. e͂. i. car. Ibi dim car. e͂ m̊. 7 dim poteft fieri.

Ibi. i. cot. Silua. xxx. porc. H̄ tra ual. xiiii. fot.

Q̨do recep. fimit. T.R.E. xx. fot. Hanc tr̄a tenuit

Turbtus ho͂ Leunini. 7 uende potuit cui uoluit.
^{comitis}

Ⓜ ROTBERT⁹ Fafiton teñ de rege. iiii. hid in Stibenhed.

Tra. e͂. iii. car. 7 ibi funt m̊. Ibi uñ uitts de. xiiii. ac.

7 alius de. xii. ac. 7 Roger⁹ uicecom. i. hid. 7 bord de

dim h̄ 7 dim uirg. Silua. lx. porc. 7 iiii. fot. Int totũ

ual. lxx. fot. Q̨do recep. fimilit. T.R.E. viii. lib.

13   LAND OF RICHARD SON OF GILBERT

ELTHORNE Hundred

1 M. Richard son of Count Gilbert holds HAREFIELD. It answers for 5
hides. Land for 5 ploughs. In lordship 2 hides; 2 ploughs there.
The villagers have 3 ploughs.
     A priest has 1 virgate; 5 villagers with 1 virgate each; 5 others,
       ½ virgate each; 7 smallholders with 5 acres each; 1 smallholder
       with 3 acres; 3 cottagers; 3 slaves.
     2 mills at 15s; from 4 fishponds, 1000 eels; meadow for 1 plough;
       pasture for the village livestock; woodland, 1200 pigs.
     Total value £12; when acquired £8; before 1066 £14.
     Countess·Goda held this manor before 1066.

14   LAND OF ROBERT GERNON

OSSULSTONE Hundred

1 M. Robert Gernon holds 2 hides in HAGGERSTON from the King. Land for 2
Land for 2 ploughs. 3 ploughs there.
     3 villagers and 7 smallholders who hold this land.
     Value 45s; when acquired 40s; before 1066, 50s.
     Alwin, King Edward's man, held this manor, and could sell to
whom he would.

In ELTHORNE Hundred

2   Nigel holds 2 hides from Robert Gernon. Land for 1 plough; ½
plough there now; ½ possible.
     1 cottager.
     Woodland, 30 pigs.
     Value of this land, 14s; when acquired the same; before 1066, 20s.
     Thorbert, Earl Leofwin's* man, held this land; he
could sell to whom he would.

15   LAND OF ROBERT [SON OF] FAFITON

OSSULSTONE Hundred

1 M. Robert [son of] Fafiton* holds 4 hides from the King in STEPNEY.
Land for 3 ploughs; they are there now.
     1 villager with 14 acres; another with 12 acres; Roger the
       Sheriff, 1 hide; a* smallholder with ½ hide and ½ virgate.
     Woodland, 60 pigs, and 4s too.
     Total value 70s; when acquired the same; before 1066 £8.

Hoc ⊕ tenuit Sired canon̄ S̃ Pauli. potuit uende̅
cui uoluit. T.R.E. Eps London̄ reclam̄ ſe habe̅ debere.
Cū his. IIII. hid ſunt m̊. LIII. ac̃ træ̃. quæ n̄ erant ibi
T.R.E. q̃s occupauit Hugo de berneres ſup̱ canonic̄
S̃ Pauli. 7 appoſuit huic Manerio. teſtante hund̄.

In Helethorne hund̄ ten̄ Rob̃t Faſiton de rege
In Ticheham. II. hid. Tra. ē. I. car̄. ſed non. ē ibi m̊.
P̃tū. I. car̄. Paſtã ad pecun uille. Silua. XXX. porc̄.
H̃ tra ual. V. ſol. Q̃do recep̃: XL. ſol. T.R.E: XL. ſobil
Hanc trã tenuit Ælmer hō Wluardi. 7 uende̅ potuit.

.XVI TERRA ROBERTI FILIJ ROZELIN OSVLVESTANE HVND.

Rotbert̃ fili Rozelini ten̄ de rege in Stibenhed
III. hid 7 dim̄. Tra. II. car̄. In dr̄io. II. hid 7 ibi eſt
.I. car̄. Villi. I. car̄. Ibi. I. uills de. I. uirg. 7 VIII. bord
q̃ſq̃ de dim̄ uirg. 7 IIII. cot. de XIX. ac̃. p̃tū. II. car̄.
7 nem ad ſepes. Int totū ual. L.III. ſol. Q̃do recep̃:
X. ſol. T.R.E: IIII. lib̃. Hanc trã tenuit Aluuin Sti
chehare ̱p uno ⊕. hō R.E. uende̅ potuit cui uoluit.

Eps Londonienſis reclamat.

.XVII. TERRA ROBERTI BLVNDI. SPELETORNE HD.

⊕ Rotbertvs blund tenet in LELEHĀ. VIII. hid.
de rege. Eſtrild q̃dã moniál ten̄ de eo. Tra. ē. V. car̄.
In dr̄io. IIII. hidæ. 7 ibi. ē. I. car̄. Villi hūt. IIII. car̄. Ibi
un uills de. I. uirg. 7 VII. uilli q̃ſq̃ dim̄ hid. 7 III. bord
de. I. uirg. 7 III. cot. P̃tū. V. car̄. Paſtã ad pec̃ uille.
In totis ualent ual. LX. ſol. Q̃do recep̃: XL. ſol. T.R.E:
VI. lib̃. Hoc ⊕ tenuit Achi Huſcarle regis. E. uende̅
potuit cui uoluit. 7 Soca jacuit in Stanes.

Sired, a Canon of St. Paul's held this manor before 1066; he could sell to whom he would. The Bishop of London claims that he ought to have it.

With these 4 hides there are now 53 acres of land, which were not there before 1066, which Hugh of Bernieres appropriated from the Canons of St. Paul's and placed in this manor, as the Hundred testifies.

In ELTHORNE Hundred

2   Robert Fafiton holds 2 hides in ICKENHAM from the King. Land for 1 plough, but it is not there now.

Meadow for 1 plough; pasture for the village livestock;   130 c
woodland, 30 pigs.

Value of this land, 5s; when acquired 40s; before 1066, 40s.*

Aelmer, Wulfward Wight's man, held this land and could sell it.

16   LAND OF ROBERT SON OF ROZELIN

OSSULSTONE Hundred

1   Robert son of Rozelin holds 3½ hides in STEPNEY from the King. Land for 2 ploughs. In lordship 2 hides; 1 plough there. The villagers, 1 plough.

1 villager with 1 virgate; 8 smallholders with ½ virgate each;
4 cottagers with 19 acres.

Meadow for 2 ploughs; wood for fences.

In total, value 53s; when acquired 10s; before 1066 £4.

Alwin Stickhare, King Edward's man, held this land as one manor; he could sell to whom he would. The Bishop of London claims it.

17   LAND OF ROBERT BLUNT*

SPELTHORNE Hundred

1   M. Robert Blunt holds 8 hides in LALEHAM from the King. Estrild, a nun, holds from him. Land for 5 ploughs. In lordship 4 hides; 1 plough there. The villagers have 4 ploughs.

1 villager with 1 virgate; 7 villagers, ½ hide each;
3 smallholders with 1 virgate; 3 cottagers.

Meadow for 5 ploughs; pasture for the village livestock.

Total value 60s; when acquired 40s; before 1066 £6.

Aki, one of King Edward's Guards, held this manor; he could sell to whom he would; the jurisdiction lay in Staines.

Ɱ ROGERIVS de Rames tenet de rege *CERDENTONE*.

ꝑ.v.hiđ ſe defđ.Tra.ē.ɪɪɪɪ.cař.In dńio.ɪɪɪɪ.hiđ.7 ɪ.cař 7 dim'

ē ibi.Viłłi diɱ cař.7 ɪɪ.cař 7 dim poſſ fieri.Ibi.ɪ.uiłłs

de dim ħ.7 ɪ.borđ de.vɪɪɪ.ac.7 vɪ.ſerui.Pťū.ɪɪɪɪ.

cař.Paſťa ad pecuɳ uille.Ħ tra uał.xxx.ſoł.Qdo

recep̓.lx.ſoł.T.R.E.̓c.ſoł.Hoc Ɱ duo frs tenueř.

un hō Stig arcħ fuit.alt hō Leuuini. comitis .uendè po

tueř cui uolueř.Soca ū ptiɳ in Stanes.

Ɱ In Hund de *GARA* teɳ iſđ Rogeri in Stanmera

ɪx.hiđ 7 dim.Tra.ē.vɪɪ.cař.In dńio.ɪɪɪɪ.hiđ.7 ɪ.cař

ibi.ē.7 ɪɪ.adhuc poſſ fieri.Viłłi hɳt.ɪɪɪ.cař.7 ɪ.plus

pot fieri.Ibi.ɪ.uiłłs de.ɪ.uirg.7 vɪɪɪ.uiłłi qſq̨ dim

uirg.7 ɪɪɪ.borđ qſq̨ de.v.ac.7 ɪɪ.ſerui.Silua octing

porc.Paſťa ad pecuɳ uillæ.7 ɪɪ.ſoł.In totis ualent

uał.lx.ſoł.Qdo recep̓.xx.ſoł.T.R.E.̓x.liƀ.Hoc Ɱ

tenuit Algar hō Heraldi. comit' .7 uendè potuit.

Ɱ Wiłłs filius anſculfi teɳ de rege.7 Hugo de eo

CRANFORDE.ꝑ v.hiđ de defđ.Tra.ē.ɪɪɪ.cař.Ibi

.ɪ.cař in dńio.7 uiłłi.ɪɪ.cař.Ibi pƀr ħt.ɪ.uirg.7 vɪɪɪ.

uiłłi quiſq̨ de.ɪ.uirg.7 ɪɪ.cot de.ɪɪ.ac.7 ɪɪɪ.ſerui.

Nem ad ſepes.Iɳt totū uał.lx.ſoł.Qdo recep̓.xl.

ſoł.T.R.E.̓c.ſoł.Hoc Ɱ tenuit Turſtin teigɳ regis.E.

7 uendè potuit cui uoluit.

18   LAND OF ROGER OF RAISMES

SPELTHORNE Hundred

1   M. Roger of Raismes holds CHARLTON from the King. It answers for 5
hides. Land for 4 ploughs. In lordship 4½ hides; 1 plough
there. The villagers, ½ plough; 2½ ploughs possible.
> 1 villager with ½ hide; 1 smallholder with 8 acres; 6 slaves.
> Meadow for 4 ploughs; pasture for the village livestock.

Value of this land, 30s; when acquired 60s; before 1066, 100s.
> Two brothers held this manor; one was Archbishop Stigand's man,
the other Earl Leofwin's man; they could sell to whom they would,
but the jurisdiction belonged to Staines.

In the Hundred of GORE

2   M. Roger also holds 9½ hides in STANMORE. Land for 7 ploughs. In
lordship 4 hides; 1 plough there; a further 2 possible. The
villagers have 3 ploughs; 1 more possible.
> 1 villager with 1 virgate; 8 villagers, ½ virgate each; 3
>   smallholders with 5 acres each; 2 slaves.
> Woodland, 800 pigs; pasture for the village livestock,
>   and 2s too.

Total value 60s; when acquired 20s; before 1066 £10.
> Algar, Earl Harold's man, held this manor and could sell.

19   LAND OF WILLIAM SON OF ANSCULF

ELTHORNE Hundred

1   M. William son of Ansculf holds CRANFORD from the King, and Hugh
from him. It answers for 5 hides. Land for 3 ploughs.
In lordship 1 plough. The villagers, 2 ploughs.
> A priest has 1 virgate; 8 villagers with 1 virgate each;
>   2 cottagers with 2 acres; 3 slaves.
> Wood for fences.

In total, value 60s; when acquired 40s; before 1066, 100s.
> Thurstan, a thane of King Edward's, held this manor and could
sell to whom he would.

.XX. TERRA EDWARDI SARISBER. OSVLVESTAN HVND.

Ⓜ Edward de Sarifberie ten CERCEHEDE *Chelched*. p̄. II. hid
Tra. ē. v. car. In dn̄io. I. hida. 7 II. car ibi funt m̄.

130 d

Vitti. I. car. 7 II. car poſſ adhuc fieri. Ibi. II. uitti de. II.
uirg. 7 IIII. uitti. qſq̃ de dim virg. 7 III. bord. qſq̃ de. v. ac.
7 III. ſerui. P̄tū. II. car. Paſta ad pecun̄ uillæ. Silua. LX.
porc. 7 LII. den. In totis ualent ual. IX. lib. Q̃do recep̄:
ſimil 7 ſēp. Hoc Ⓜ tenuit Wluuene hō regis. E. potuit
uende cui uoluit.

.XXI. TERRA ALBERICI DE VER. OSVLVESTANE HVND.

Ⓜ Albericvs de uer ten de epo conſtantienſi *Chenesit*.
p̄ x. hid ſe defd̄. Tra. ē. x. car. Ibi in dn̄io ſunt. IIII. car.
7 vitti hn̄t v. car. 7 VI. pot fieri. Ibi. XII. uitti. qſq̃. I. uirg.
7 VI. uitti de. III. uirg. P̄br dim uirg. 7 VII. ſerui. P̄tū. II.
car. Paſta ad pecun̄ uillæ. Silua. cc. porc. 7 III. Arpenn
uineæ. In totis ualent ual. x. lib. Q̃do recep̄: VI. lib. T.R.E.
x. lib. Hoc Ⓜ tenuit Eduuin teign regis. E. 7 uende potuit.

.XXII. TERRA RANÑ FRIS ILGERIJ. OSVLVESTANE HVND.

Rannvlf fr̄ Ilgerij. ten de rege *Tolentone*. p̄. II. hid.
Tra. ē. II. car. In dn̄io. I. hid. 7 ibi. ē. I. car. Vitti hn̄t. II. car.
Ibi. v. uitti qſq̃ de dim uirg. 7 II. bord. de. IX. ac. 7 I. cot
7 I. ſeruus. Paſta ad pec̄ uillæ. Silua. LX. porc. 7 v. ſolid.
Ħ tra ual. XL. ſol. Q̃do recep̄: LX. ſol. T.R.E. XL. ſol. Hanc
tenuit Edduin hō regis. E. 7 uende potuit.

.XXIII. TERRA DERMAN LVNDON. OSVLVESTANE HVND.

Derman ten de rege in *Iseldone* dim hid. Tra. ē dim car.
Ibi. ē un uitts. Ħ tra ual 7 ualuit. x. ſol. Hanc tra te
nuit Algar hō regis. E. 7 uende 7 dare potuit.

20   LAND OF EDWARD OF SALISBURY

OSSULSTONE Hundred

1   M. Edward of Salisbury holds CHELSEA for 2 hides. Land for 5 ploughs.
In lordship 1 hide; 2 ploughs there now. The villagers, 1 plough;   130 d
a further 2 ploughs possible.
     2 villagers with 2 virgates; 4 villagers with ½ virgate each;
       3 smallholders with 5 acres each; 3 slaves.
     Meadow for 2 ploughs; pasture for the village livestock;
       woodland, 60 pigs, and 52d too.
   Total value £9; when acquired and always the same.
   Wulfwen, King Edward's man,* held this manor; she could
sell to whom she would.

21   LAND OF AUBREY DE VERE

OSSULSTONE Hundred

1   M. Aubrey de Vere holds KENSINGTON from the Bishop of Coutances.
It answers for 10 hides. Land for 10 ploughs. In lordship 4
ploughs. The villagers have 5 ploughs; 6 possible.*
     12 villagers, 1 virgate each; 6 villagers with 3 virgates;
       a priest, ½ virgate; 7 slaves.
     Meadow for 2 ploughs; pasture for the village livestock;
       woodland, 200 pigs; 3 *arpents* of vines.
   Total value £10; when acquired £6; before 1066 £10.
   Edwin, a thane of King Edward's, held this manor and could sell.

22   LAND OF RANULF BROTHER OF ILGER

OSSULSTONE Hundred

1   Ranulf brother of Ilger holds TOLLINGTON* from the King for 2 hides.
Land for 2 ploughs. In lordship 1 hide; 1 plough there. The
villagers have 2 ploughs.
     5 villagers with ½ virgate each; 2 smallholders with 9 acres;
       1 cottager; 1 slave.
     Pasture for the village livestock; woodland, 60 pigs, and 5s too.
   Value of this land, 40s; when acquired 60s; before 1066, 40s.
   Edwin, King Edward's man, held this (land) and could sell.

23   LAND OF DERMAN OF LONDON

OSSULSTONE Hundred

1   Derman holds ½ hide in ISLINGTON from the King. Land for ½ plough.
     1 villager.
   The value of this land is and was 10s.
   Algar, King Edward's man, held this land and could sell or grant it.

Ⓜ JVDITA comitiſſa teñ *TOTEHAM* de rege. p. v. hiḍ ſe defḍ
Tra.e̅.x.car̅. In dñio ſuɴ carucatæ træ p̅t has.v.hiḍ.

7 ibi funt.II.car̅. Vitti hñt.XII.car̅. P̅br h̅t dim̅ hiḍ.7 VI.
uitti de.VI.uirg̅.7 XXIIII.uitti qſq̣ de dim̅ uirg̅.7 XII.borḍ.
qſq̣ de.v.ac̅.7 XVII.cot. Ibi.II.francig̅ de.I.hiḍ 7 IIII.uirg̅.
7 IIII.ſerui. p̅tu̅.x.car̅.7 XX.ſot deſup plus. Paſta ad pec̃
uille. Silua q̃ngent porc̃. De.I.gort.III.ſot. In totis
ualent uat.XXV.lib̅.7 XV.ſot.7 III.unc̃ auri. Q̃do recep̅:
x.lib̅. T.R.E.́ xxvI.lib̅. Hoc Ⓜ tenuit Wallef comes.

Ⓜ LILESTONE. p v. hiḍ ſe defḍ. Eideua tenet de rege.
Tra.e̅.III.car̅. In dñio.IIII.hiḍ 7 dim̅.7 ibi ſuɴ. t̅I.car̅.
Vitti hñt.I.car̅. Ibi.IIII.uitti qſq̣ de dim̅ uirg̅.7 III.cot
de.II.ac̃.7 I.ſeruus. p̅tu̅.I.car̅. Paſta ad pec̃ uillæ.
Silua.c.porc̃. De herbagia.III.den̅. In totis ualent uat
LX.ſot. Q̃do recep̅: ſimilit. T.R.E.́ XL.ſot. Hoc Ⓜ tenuit
Eduuard hō regis.E.7 uendḛ potuit.

F. Suani. 9

In hund de Spelethorne ten̅ Ælueue fem̅ Wateman de Lond'
de rege dim̅ hiḍ.7 III. part̅ dim̅ hiḍ. Tra.IIII.boḇ. ſ̣ n̅ ſ ibi.
p̅tu̅.IIII.boḇ. Paſta ad pec̃ uillæ. Int̅ totu̅ uat 7 ualuit
IIII.ſot. Hanc tr̅a tenuit Aluuin. hō Leuuini.7 uendḛ potuit.
De hac tra Goiſt̅ de manneuile erat ſaiſit. qdo iuit
tranſmare in ſeruitiu̅ regis. ut dñt hōes ſui 7 tot̅ hundret.
In Hvnd de Helethorne ten̅ Ælueue in Greneforde
dim̅ hiḍ de rege. Tra.e̅ dim̅ car̅. ſ; n̅.e̅ ibi m̅. H̅ tra
uat x.ſot. Q̃do recep̅: ſimit. T.R.E.́ xx.ſot. Hanc tram
tenuit Leuric hō Leuuini.7 uendḛ potuit cui uoluit.

LAND OF THE COUNTESS JUDITH

EDMONTON Hundred

1 M. The Countess Judith holds TOTTENHAM from the King. It answers for 5
hides. Land for 10 ploughs. In lordship 2 carucates of land, besides
these 5 hides*; 2 ploughs there. The villagers have 12 ploughs.

A priest has ½ hide; 6 villagers with 6 virgates; 24 villagers
with ½ virgate each; 12 smallholders with 5 acres each; 17
cottagers; 2 Frenchmen with 1 hide and 3 virgates; 4 slaves.

Meadow for 10 ploughs, and 20s over and above; pasture for the
village livestock; woodland, 500 pigs; from 1 weir, 3s.

Total value £25 15s, and 3 ounces of gold; when acquired £10;
before 1066 £26.

Earl Waltheof held this manor.

25 ## LAND GIVEN IN ALMS*

OSSULSTONE Hundred

1 M. LISSON* answers for 5 hides. Edeva holds it from the King.
Land for 3 ploughs. In lordship 4½ hides; 2 ploughs there.
The villagers have 1 plough.

4 villagers with ½ virgate each; 3 cottagers with 2 acres; 1 slave.

Meadow for 1 plough; pasture for the village livestock;
woodland, 100 pigs; from grazing, 3d.

Total value 60s; when acquired the same; before 1066, 40s.

Edward son of Swein, King Edward's man, held this manor
and could sell.

In the Hundred of SPELTHORNE

2 Aelfeva, the wife of Hwaetmann of London, holds ½ hide and the
third part of ½ hide from the King. Land for 4 oxen, but they
are not there.

Meadow for 4 oxen; pasture for the village livestock.

In total, the value is and was 4s.

Alwin White, Earl Leofwin's man, held this land and
could sell. Geoffrey de Mandeville was put in possession of
this land when he went across the sea in the King's service;
as his men and the whole Hundred state.

In the Hundred of ELTHORNE

3 Aelfeva holds ½ hide in GREENFORD from the King. Land for ½ plough,
but it is not there now.

Value of this land, 10s; when acquired the same; before 1066, 20s.

Leofric, Earl Leofwin's man, held this land and could sell
to whom he would.

Blank folio   131 a-d

ABBREVIATIONS used in the notes.

DB..Domesday Book. MS.. Manuscript. EPNS..English Place Names Society.*
VCH..Victoria County History.* EHR..English Historical Review. PNDB..
O. von Feilitzen *The Pre-Conquest Personal Names of Domesday Book*
Uppsala 1937.† OEB..G. Tengvik *Old English Bynames* Uppsala 1938.†

* refers to the County volume, unless otherwise stated.
+ 'Nomina Germanica,' volumes 3 and 4.

The manuscript is written on leaves, or folios, of parchment (sheep-skin), measuring about
15 inches by 11 (38 by 28 cm), on both sides. On each side, or page, are two columns,
making four to each folio. The folios were numbered in the 17th century, and the four
columns of each are here lettered a,b,c,d, marked in the margin. The manuscript emphasises
words and usually distinguishes chapters and sections by the use of red ink. Underlining
in black ink, indicates deletion.

MIDDLESEX. In red, across the top of the page, spread above both. *'Midelsexe'* pages
127 a,b - 130 c,d; omitted 126 d and blank pages.
Blank columns. All or most of these five columns, and the top three quarters of 126 d,
were probably reserved for the Survey of London, which was never transcribed.

1,1	OSSULSTONE. The stone stood in what is now Park Lane in 1484; on its east side, near its junction with South Street, in 1614 (EPNS 81); probably identical with the stone (?) 'where soldiers are shot' at Tyburn (now Marble Arch), marked on Rocque's *Map of London,* 1746 (Sheet A 2); replaced beside the Marble Arch between the 1870s and the 1890s, but subsequently removed. It was evidently of considerable size. 'Oswulf's Stone', presumably named after an early English settler, was probably the meeting place of the Hundred; it may have been of Roman origin.
2,1	FRENCHMEN. *Franc.* Not here *franci* (free). The phrase recurs in 2,2; 3,12; 5,1; 10,1; 11,1-2; 12,1. In each of these 8 entries, *Francig(enae)* (Frenchmen) or *milites* (men-at-arms) are listed, and in 12,1 the Frenchman is identified as a man-at-arms. Frenchmen also occur, without this preliminary heading, in 4,8 and 7,6.
	PLOUGH. Meaning sufficient meadow for the 8 oxen who drew the plough.
	PIGS. The Latin may mean either sufficient woodland to pasture 400 etc. pigs, or woodland on which 400 etc. pigs are paid for right of pasture. In Middlesex, the 'third pig' was paid at Chalkhill in Kingsbury about 1045 (F.E. Harmer *Anglo-Saxon Writs* Manchester 1952. no. 77, p.344 = Kemble 843), and the high payment of one pig in three for pasturage may have been in force elsewhere in the county.
3,2	IN THE SAME VILLAGE. The words are repeated at the beginning of sections 3,2 - 3,11.
	BEFORE 1066. Probably refers grammatically to Sired, see 3,4 - 3,6 below; but in practice also refers to the Canons and Doding.
3,7	BISHOP OF LISIEUX. Gilbert Maminot, the King's doctor and chaplain.
3,15	OSSULSTONE HUNDRED. The Hundred heading is repeated after the long account of the Bishop's manor of Fulham, itself in Ossulstone, because it begins a separate list of the Canons' holdings, whose equivalent in some counties is entered as a separate chapter of the Survey.
3,18	MANOR. *p(ro) i M(anerio) de v hid(is)* (as one manor of 5 hides) was written first; *pro* (above the line) and *se def(en)d(it)* (at the end of the line, protruding into the margin) were added later, meaning 'it answers for 5 hides'. The down-stroke of the 'p', shown as a separate line by Farley, is carried well below the line in the MS, to indicate deletion.

	ANSWERS. *se defendit.* Grammatically, either 'answers' or 'answered'.
3,19	RUG MOOR. In or about the district that was renamed Camden Town in 1795 EPNS 142, see also 141.
3,30	ELTHORNE..DRAYTON. As the text stands, in Ossulstone Hundred, and therefore Drayton in Ealing (TQ 16 80), EPNS 91. St. Paul's held a Drayton from at least the 10th century, but later in the middle ages its holding was distinguished as West Drayton. It is **theoretically** possible that the 1066 holding meant Drayton in Ealing, but more probable that a Hundred heading has been omittted from the text, and that West Drayton was intended.
4,5	THE ABBOT..HOLDS. These words are repeated, after the place name, in each of the sections 4,5 - 4,10.
	3 COTTAGERS. A second '7' ('and') is written over the first 'i' of 'iii'; a space equivalent to 3 or 4 letters is left between *cot'* and *de* (cottagers with).
6,1	TYBURN. Including much of Marylebone, see EPNS 137.
7,5	COLHAM. At and near Colham Green, Hillingdon.
7,7	AELFETH. Alfit, see OEB 131.
8,2	THE COUNT ALSO HOLDS. These words are repeated, after the place name, in each of the sections 8,2 - 8,6.
8,4	8 PLOUGHS. The figures do not agree; it may be that '9 ploughs' were accidentally subtracted from '12 hides' instead of '10 ploughs'; see also 12,1 and 21,1.
8,6	ATOR. The commoner spelling of the name. The meaning is perhaps 'venomous', or 'dreadful', OEB 341; PNDB 232-233.
9,1	EBURY. At or near Ebury Square, Victoria, S.W.1.
9,3	WULFBERT. So PNDB 418.
9,6	HELD. A misprint in many copies of Farley omits the first letter of *tenuerunt.*
9,9	LORDS'. *Dominorum,* plural.
11,4	VILLAGERS. MS *ii virg' de i virg'* written in error for *ii vill' de i virg'.*
12,1	11. The figures do not agree; an 'x' (10) has perhaps been omitted; see 8,4 and 21,1.
	PROVEN. The exact meaning is uncertain.
12,2	HAMPTON. In Spelthorne Hundred in later records; it is possible that a Hundred heading has been omitted.
14,2	LEOFWIN. MS *Leuuini;* Farley *Leunini* in error.
15,1	[SON OF] FAFITON. So in Hunts. 25,1(207 b).
	A. The 'b' of *bord(ar)* is written over a figure, perhaps *ii* or *v*; 2 smallholders with 75 acres would mean improbably large holdings, and the figure 5 is therefore more credible; but the figure may have been deliberately overwritten, to mean, the smallholders, their number unstated, if the figure in the return copied was rejected as wrong, while the proper figure was not known.
15,2	40s. Farley *'sobil'.* The MS has been corrected from *sol(idos),* shillings, to *simil(iter),* likewise.
17,1	BLUNT. *Blundus,* 'blonde', the origin of the modern surname. Elsewhere in DB Robert is sometimes called *Albus* or *Blancardus,* 'white', or *Flavus,* 'yellow' or 'fair'.
20,1	MAN. *Homo,* Here including women.
21,1	6 POSSIBLE. If six is read, the figures do not agree; perhaps *ta* turning *sex* to *sexta* was omitted; see 8,4 and 12,1.
22,1	TOLLINGTON. About Tollington Place, Finsbury Park, N.4.
24,1	BESIDES..HIDES. As in Huntingdonshire, Hurstingstone Hundred, (see Hunts. B 21, note), where the lordship ploughs are exempt from tax. *Carucatae,* not otherwise used in Middlesex, may be a mistaken expansion of a *car* or *c'* in the original return, which, as in Huntingdonshire, may have intended *carucae,* ploughs.
25	IN ALMS. Comparable chapters in other counties have the headings 'The King's Thanes', 'The King's Servants', and the like.
25,1	LISSON. At or near Lisson Grove, Marylebone, N.W.1.

Middlesex is the only county whose survey systematically lists the size of the holdings of villagers and others who are counted but not named. The table below gives for each class the range of holdings, from the largest to the smallest recorded in the county, and the average holding. Figures in brackets give the reference to the largest and smallest holdings. The size is given in acres, on the Domesday reckoning of 120 acres to the hide, 30 acres to the virgate; the average is given to the nearest round figure, and its equivalent in hides and virgates is also given.

	extremes	average acres	hides and virgates	Reference
Men-at-arms and Frenchmen	270 to 97½	180	1½ hides	(2,1; 10,1)
Villagers	150 to 10	30	1 virgate	(4,8; 3,22)
Smallholders	20 to 2/3	7½	¼ virgate	(4,8; 3,3)
Cottagers with land	4 to 1/3	1	-	(5,5; 3,24)
All cottagers	4 to nil	under ½	-	-

The range of all classes overlap; the richest villagers held more land than the poorest men-at-arms, the richest smallholders more than the poorest villagers, the richest cottagers more than the poorest smallholder. But the majority of each class was much nearer to the average than to the extreme, so that the averages sharply distinguish the classes; on average, the man-at-arms had six times the villager's holding, the villager 4 times the smallholder's, the smallholder 6 or 8 times the landed cottager's; and three out of every five cottagers are entered with no land, save for a few 'with their gardens'.

The survey also lists the size of holdings of Freemen (*sochemanni*) in or before 1066. They correspond closely to those of the men-at-arms and Frenchmen, the wealthiest local class, ranging from 240 to 60 acres (7,4 and 9,4 and 11,3; 11,2), with an average of 150 acres (1¼ hides). Their social status, appropriate to their substantial holdings, is sufficiently evidenced by the notice (9,4) that one of them was a Canon of St. Paul's.

It cannot be assumed that the Middlesex figures are typical of the whole country. But elsewhere numerous figures listed unsystematically suggest that in many counties the average holdings of the various classes did not greatly differ. The fuller detail given for Middlesex provides a yardstick against which differences and similarities may be measured.

INDEX OF PERSONS

Familiar modern spellings are given when they exist. Unfamiliar names are usually given in an approximate late 11th century form, avoiding variants that were already obsolescent or pedantic. Spellings that mislead the modern eye are avoided where possible. Two, however, cannot be avoided; they are combined in the name 'Leofgeat,' pronounced 'Leffyet,' or 'Levyet.' The definite article is omitted before bynames, except when there is reason to suppose that they described the individual. The chapter numbers of listed landholders are printed in italics.

Ranulf brother of Ilger	22	Ulf, King Edward's thane	7,6
Richard	11,2	Ulf son of Manni	7,8
Richard son of Count Gilbert	13	Canon Walter	3,29
Robert Blunt	17	Walter of Mucedent	11,3-4
Robert [son of] Fafiton	15	Walter of St. Valery	12
Robert Gernon	14	Walter son of Othere	11
Robert son of Rozelin	16	Earl Waltheof	24,1
Robert	7,2	Wight, see Wulfward	
Earl Roger	7	Wigot	7,3-5; 7
Sheriff Roger	3,3. 15,1	Bishop William	3,3 9; 11
Roger of Raismes	18	William the Chamberlain	1,4. 3,8
Rozelin, see Robert			4,11. 9,1
Canon Sired	3,2. 15,1	William de Vere	3,5
Stickhare, see Alwin		William son of Ansculf	19
Archbishop Stigand	2,1. 18,1	Wulfbert	9,3
Swein, see Edward		Wulfward Wight	8,5. 10,1-2
Thorbert, Earl Leofwin's man	2,3. 14,2		15,2
Thurstan	19,1	Wulfward	7,8
Toki	7,8	Wulfwen	20,1
Ulf, King Edward's Guard	7,2	wife of Brian	3,3

Churches and Clergy

Archbishop of Canterbury 2 (see also Lanfranc, Stigand). Bishop of Coutances 21,1; of Lisieux 3,7; of London 3; 15,1; 16,1 (see also William). Abbess of Barking 6. Abbot of Chertsey 8,2; of Fecamp 8,1; of Holy Trinity, Rouen 5; of Westminster 4. Canons of St. Paul's 3,2; 14-30. 9,4. 15,1 (see also Durand, Englebert, Gyrth, Ralph, Sired, Walter). Nun, see Estrild. St. Paul's, see Bishop of London; St. Peter's, see Abbot of Westminster.

Secular Titles

Chamberlain (*Camerarius*)...William. Constable (*Stalrus*)...Asgar. Count (*Comes*)...Gilbert; of Mortain. Earl (*Comes*)...Algar; Harold; Leofwin; Ralph; Roger; Waltheof. Queen (*Regina*)... Edith. Reeve (*Prefectus*)...8,1. Sheriff (*Vicecomes*)...Roger; King's Sheriff 1,3-4; Sheriff of Middlesex 1,3. Thane (*Teignus*)...Alwin Horne; Edmer Ator; Edwin; Thurstan; Ulf; Wulfward Wight.

INDEX OF PLACES

The name of each place is followed by (i) the initial of its Hundred and its location on the Map in this volume; (ii) its National Grid reference; (iii) chapter and section references in DB. Bracketed figures denote mention in sections dealing with a different place. Unless otherwise stated, the identifications of the English Place Names Society and the spellings of the Ordnance Survey are followed for places in England; of OEB for places abroad. The National Grid reference system is explained on all Ordnance Survey maps, and in the Automobile Association Handbooks; the figures reading from left to right are given before those reading from bottom to top of the map. Italics denote unidentifiable names; inverted commas enclose obsolete or lost names. All places in Middlesex named in DB, except South Mimms, are in the 100 kilometre grid square TQ. The Middlesex Hundreds are Edmonton (Ed); Elthorne (E); Gore (G); Hounslow (later called Isleworth) (H); Ossulstone (O); Spelthorne (S).

Ashford	S 6	07 71	8,2	Dawley	E 11	09 79	7,7
(East) Bedfont	S 3	08 73	8,3; 11,2	(West) Drayton	E 10	06 79	3,30
West Bedfont	S 3	07 74	11,3	Ebury	O 20	28 78	9,1
Bishopsgate	O 15	33 81	3,27	Edmonton	Ed 3	33 92	9,8
(Camden Town)*	O	see—Rug Moor		Enfield	Ed 2	32 96	9,9
Charlton	S 8	08 69	18,1	Feltham	S 4	10 73	8,3-4
Chelsea	O 21	27 78	20,1	Fulham	O 22	24 76	3,12-14
Colham	E 6	06 81	7,5; (1-3; 7-8)	Greenford	E 8	14 82	4,8; 9,4-5; 25,3
Cowley	E 5	05 82	4,10	Haggerston	O 10	34 83	14,1
Cranford	E 15	10 77	19,1	Hampstead	O 2	26 85	4,3-4

Hampton	H 2	13 69	12 2		(Marylebone)*	O	–	–
Hanwell	E 12	16 79	4,9		(South) Mimms	Ed 1	†22 01	(9,8)
Hanworth	S 7	11 71	7,2		(Stoke) Newington	O 3	33 86	3,24
Harefield	E 1	05 90	13,1		*Nomansland*	O	–	1,1
Harlesden	O 6	21 83	3,18		Northolt	E 4	12 84	9,7
Harlington	E 14	08 77	7,4		'Rug Moor'	O 7	29 83	3,19
Harmondsworth	E 13	05 77	5,1. 7,3		Ruislip	E 2	09 86	10,1
Harrow	G 2	15 89	2,2; (3)		St. Pancras	O 12	30 83	3,21; 29
Hatton	S 1	09 75	2,1		Shepperton	S12	08 67	4,7
Hayes	E 9	10 80	2,1		Staines	S 5	03 71	4,5; (8,1; 2.
Hendon	G 3	21 89	4,12					17,1; 18,1)
Hillingdon	E 7	06 82	7,6		*Stanestaple*	O	–	3,28
Holborn	O 14	31 81	1,1		Stanmore	G 1	16 92	8,6; 18,2
Hoxton	O 9	33 83	3,25-26		Stanwell	S 2	05 74	11,1; (2)
Ickenham	E 3	07 86	7,8; 9,6; 15,2		Stepney	O 16	35 81	3,1-11; 15,1;
Isleworth	H 1	16 75	12,1					16,1
Islington	O 8	31 84	3,22-23; 9,3;		Sunbury	S 11	10 68	4,6
			23,1		Tollington	O 1	30 85	22,1
Kempton	S 9	10 70	8,5; (2)		Tottenham	Ed 4	33 90	24,1
Kensington	O 17	24 79	21,1		Tottenham (Court)	O 11	29 82	3,20
Kingsbury	G 4	20 88	4,11; 10,2		Twyford	O 5	18 83	3,15-16
Laleham	S 10	05 68	8,1; 17,1		Tyburn	O 18	27 80	6,1
Lisson	O 13	27 82	25,1		Willesden	O 4	22 84	3,17
London*	O	32 81	3,12		Westminster	O 19	30 79	4,1-2

Camden Town, see Rug Moor; *London*, see also Index of Persons, Bishop, Derman, Hwaetman;
Marylebone, see Lisson, Tyburn. † Grid Square TL.

Places not named: In ELTHORNE Hundred, 2,3; 14,2. In OSSULSTONE Hundred, 9,2.
In SPELTHORNE Hundred, 5,2; 25,2.

Places not in Middlesex (see Index of Persons)

Elsewhere in Britain
ESSEX Barking ... Abbess. KENT Canterbury ... Archbishop. SURREY Chertsey ... Abbot.
WILTSHIRE Salisbury ... Edward.

Outside Britain
Bernieres ... Hugh. Coutances ... Bishop. Fecamp ... Abbot. Hesdin ... Arnulf. Lisieux ... Bishop.
Lorraine ... Albert. Mandeville ... Geoffrey. Mortain ... Count. Mucedent ... Walter. Raismes ...
Roger. Rouen ... Abbot. St. Valery ... Walter. Ver(e) ... Aubrey, William.

SYSTEMS OF REFERENCE TO DOMESDAY BOOK

The manuscript is divided into numbered chapters, and the chapters into sections, usually
marked by large initials and red ink. Farley however did not number the sections. References
in the past have therefore been to the page or column. Several different ways of referring to
the same column have been in use. The commonest are:

(i)	(ii)	(iii)	(iv)	(v)
152 a	152	152 a	152	152 ai
152 b	152	152 a	152.2	152 a2
152 c	152 b	152 b	152 b	152 bi
152 d	152 b	152 b	152 b.2	152 b2

The relation between Vinogradoff's notation (i), here followed, and the sections is

127 a	1,1-2,2		129 a	7,1-7,7
b	2,3-3,4		b	7,8-8,5
c	3,4-3,12		c	8,6-9,6
d	3,13-3,19		d	9,6-10,2
128 a	3,20-3,29		130 a	10,2-12,1
b	3,29-4,5		b	12,1-15,2
c	4,5-4,10		c	15,2-20,1
d	4,10-6,1		d	20,1-25,3

KEY TO THE MAP

EDMONTON Hundred

1 (South) Mimms
2 Enfield
3 Edmonton
4 Tottenham

ELTHORNE Hundred

1 Harefield
2 Ruislip
3 Ickenham
4 Northolt
5 Cowley
6 Colham
7 Hillingdon
8 Greenford
9 Hayes
10 West Drayton
11 Dawley
12 Hanwell
13 Harmondsworth
14 Harlington
15 Cranford

GORE Hundred

1 Stanmore
2 Harrow
3 Hendon
4 Kingsbury

HOUNSLOW Hundred

1 Isleworth
2 Hampton

OSSULSTONE Hundred

1 Tollington
2 Hampstead
3 (Stoke) Newington
4 Willesden
5 Twyford
6 Harlesdon
7 'Rug Moor'
8 Islington
9 Hoxton
10 Haggerston
11 Tottenham (Court)
12 St. Pancras
13 Lisson
14 Holborn
15 Bishopsgate
16 Stepney
17 Kensington
18 Tyburn
19 Westminster
20 Ebury
21 Chelsea
22 Fulham

Not mapped

'Nomansland'
Stanestaple

SPELTHORNE Hundred

1 Hatton
2 Stanwell
3 Bedfont
4 Feltham
5 Staines
6 Ashford
7 Hanworth
8 Charlton
9 Kempton
10 Laleham
11 Sunbury
12 Shepperton

National Grid figures are shown on the map border.

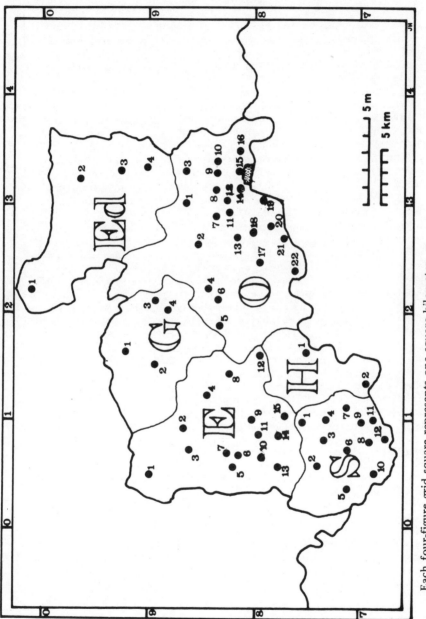

Each four-figure grid square represents one square kilometer, or 247 acres, approximately 2 hides, at 120 acres to the hide,

On the scale of this map, each dot is equivalent to about 100 acres.

TECHNICAL TERMS

Many words meaning measurements have to be transliterated. But translation may not dodge other problems by the use of obsolete or made-up words which do not exist in modern English. The translations here used are given in italics. They cannot be exact; they aim at the nearest modern equivalent. Words of uncertain or arguable meaning are marked with a star (*).

ARPENT.* A measure of extent, usually of vineyards. *a r p e n t*

BORDARIUS. Cultivator of inferior status, usually with a little land. *s m a l l h o l d e r*

CARUCA. A plough, with the oxen who pulled it, usually reckoned as 8. *p l o u g h*

CARUCATA. Normally the equivalent of a *hide*, in former Danish areas. *c a r u c a t e*

COTARIUS. Inhabitant of a *cote*, cottage, often without land. *c o t t a g e r*

DOMINICUS.* Belonging to a lord or lordship. *t h e   l o r d ' s* or *h o u s e h o l d*

DOMINIUM.* The mastery or dominion of a lord *(dominus)*; including ploughs, land, men, villages, etc., reserved for the lord's use; often concentrated in a *home farm* or *demesne*, a 'Manor Farm' or 'Lordship Farm'. *l o r d s h i p*

FEUDUM.* Continental variant of *feuum*, not used in England before 1066; either a landholder's total holding, or land held by special grant. *H o l d i n g*

FEUUM. Old English *feoh*, cattle, money, possessions in general, compare Latin *pecunia* and German *Vieh*; in later centuries, *feoff*, 'fief' or 'fee'. *h o l d i n g*

FIRMA. Old English *feorm*, provisions due to the King; a fixed sum paid in place of these and of other miscellaneous dues. *r e v e n u e*

GELDUM. The principal royal tax, originally levied during the Danish wars, normally at an equal number of pence on each *hide* of land. *t a x*

HIDE.* A unit of land measurement, reckoned at 120 acres, but often defferent in practice; a unit of tax assessment, often differing from the cultivated hides. *h i d e*

HUNDRED. A district within a shire, whose assembly of notables and village representatives usually met about once a month. *H u n d r e d*

M. Marginal abbreviation for *manerium*, manor. *M.*

PRAEPOSITUS, PRAEFECTUS. Old English *gerefa*, a royal officer. *r e e v e*

SOCA.* *'Soke'*, from *socn*, to seek, comparable with Latin *quaestio*. Jurisdiction, with the right to receive fines and a multiplicity of other dues. District in which such *soca* is exercised; a place in a *soca*. *j u r i s d i c t i o n*

SOCMANNUS.* *'Soke man,'* liable to attend the court of a *soca* and serve its lords; free from many villagers' burdens; before 1066 often with more land and higher status than villagers (see, e.g., Middlesex, Appendix); bracketed in the Commissioners' brief with the *liber homo* (free man). *F r e e m a n*

TAINUS, TEGNUS. Person holding land from the King by special grant; in former times used of the King's chief ministers and companions. *t h a n e*

T.R.E. *tempore regis Edwardi*, in King Edward's time. *b e f o r e   1 0 6 6*

VILLA. Translating Old English *tun*, town. The later distinction between a small *village* and a large *town* was not yet in use in 1086. *v i l l a g e*

VILLANUS. Member of a *villa*. *v i l l a g e r*

VIRGATA. A fraction of a *hide*, usually a quarter, notionally 30 acres. *v i r g a t e*.